FERGUSON CAREER BIOGRAPHIES

LAURA BUSH

Teacher, Librarian, and First Lady

Dina E. Forbes

Ferguson
An imprint of ☑️ Facts On File

Laura Bush: Teacher, Librarian, and First Lady

Copyright © 2005 by Facts On File, Inc.

All rights reserved. No part of this book may be reproduced or utilized in any form or by any means, electronic or mechanical, including photocopying, recording, or by any information storage or retrieval systems, without permission in writing from the publisher. For information contact

Ferguson
An imprint of Facts On File, Inc.
132 West 31st Street
New York NY 10001

Library of Congress Cataloging-in-Publication Data
Forbes, Dina E.
    Laura Bush : teacher, librarian, and First Lady/Dina E. Forbes.
       p. cm.
    Includes bibliographical references and index.
    ISBN 0-8160-5886-5 (hc : alk. paper)
  1. Bush, Laura Welch, 1946–Juvenile literature.   2. Presidents' spouses—United States—Biography—Juvenile literature.   3. Teachers—United States—Biography—Juvenile literature.   4. Librarians—United States—Biography—Juvenile literature.
5. Vocational guidance—United States—Juvenile literature.   I. Title.
    E904.B87F67   2005
    973.931'092—dc22
                                                                                                2004008819

Ferguson books are available at special discounts when purchased in bulk quantities for businesses, associations, institutions, or sales promotions. Please call our Special Sales Department in New York at (212) 967-8800 or (800) 322-8755.

You can find Ferguson on the World Wide Web at http://www.fergpubco.com

Text design by David Strelecky

Pages 92–128 adapted from Ferguson's *Encyclopedia of Careers and Vocational Guidance, Twelfth Edition.*

Printed in the United States of America

MB TB   10 9 8 7 6 5 4 3 2 1

This book is printed on acid-free paper.

CONTENTS

1	The Teacher from Texas	1
2	Growing Up in Midland	5
3	From College Student to Career Woman	19
4	Marriage and Family	29
5	First Lady of Texas	47
6	First Lady of the United States	61
7	A New Challenge	77
	Time Line	88

How to Become an Elementary School Teacher	92
To Learn More about Elementary School Teachers	105
How to Become a Librarian	107
To Learn More about Librarians	126
To Learn More about Laura Bush	129
Index	133

1

THE TEACHER FROM TEXAS

"I've never given a speech before this many people before, but I feel very at home in this classroom setting. Education is the living room of my life."

With those words, Laura Welch Bush set the tone for what was at the time her largest audience ever. She was giving a speech at the 2000 Republican National Convention. It would have been a major accomplishment for any American, but it was an especially remarkable feat for Laura; the woman from Texas was extremely shy. In fact, she was so shy that her husband, George W. Bush, had promised her before their marriage that she would never have to make a political speech. That promise was broken, however, only two months after their wedding day. George was unable to attend a political rally, so Laura gave a speech on his behalf. Afterward, George explained that his wife was not used to speaking in public. "My wife's a librarian," he joked. "Her idea of making a speech is 'Shhhh!'"

Laura's speech at the Republican National Convention was especially significant for two reasons. First, it demonstrated her passion for a cause that she would continue to speak about after she became first lady of the United States: education. Also, it was an example of her willingness to do her best to help others without complaining, even when it involved doing something that made her uncomfortable.

It was not the first speech Laura Bush had ever made, and it would certainly not be the last. Laura has made many speeches about the importance of literacy, the ability to read and write. And she still speaks out on that topic and many others today. She supports projects such as Ready to Read, Ready to Learn, which helps children start reading at an early age. She also speaks out about the No Child Left Behind Act. This program tries to find and use information about the best ways to teach reading.

But no matter how good the projects are, Laura understands that they cannot be effective without a very important component: teachers. Teachers, Laura says, "are helping to shape our children's future and our future. For that we owe them our highest regard, our highest respect." So Laura also promotes projects that recruit people to become quality teachers. The Teach for America program, for example, recruits recent college graduates to teach in inner-city communities and rural areas, where they are needed the most. The Troops to Teachers program helps people in the military become teachers. And the New Teacher Project asks the best professionals in the country to be teachers.

Another issue important to Laura is women's health. She says about women, "We're very quick to take care of our husbands, children, and family, but very slow to take care of ourselves." For this reason, she supports programs that teach people about the risks of heart disease, the number one killer of women. She is also active in educating women about breast cancer.

Laura Bush started out making a difference in her home state, when her husband was governor of Texas. Since she became first lady of the United States, she has been an important force in programs that affect the entire country. But her positive influence has not stopped there: She also tries to help people in other countries throughout the world. In November 2001, Laura became the first first lady in history to record a full presidential radio address. In that radio speech, she told the world about the cruel treatment of women and children by the government in Afghanistan, a country about 7,000 miles away from the United States. She wanted the United States to help the people in Afghanistan who could not help themselves.

This is the story of how a simple, quiet young girl from Texas grew up to be a noteworthy woman whose voice would be heard around the world.

Although she is a quiet person by nature, Laura has made many public speeches on subjects ranging from literacy to women's health. (Landov)

2

GROWING UP IN MIDLAND

Virtually from the day of her birth, the daughter of Harold and Jenna Welch had a pleasant and calming presence. "She never cried and she was hardly ever sick," says Laura's mother, calling her only child "a happy little kiddo."

Laura Lane Welch was born to Harold and Jenna Welch on November 4, 1946. She was born and raised in Midland, a town in west Texas. Today, almost 100,000 people live in Midland. However, the town was very different when Laura was growing up. She remembers it as "a small town in a vast desert, a place where neighbors had to help each other because any other help was too far away." Midland played an important role in forming the values that Laura would have for the rest of her life. "Midland was a place of family and community, and it had a sense of possibility as big as the west Texas sky," Laura says. "Midland formed value reserves as deep [as] and longer lasting than any of its oil wells."

Two other factors influenced Midland as well: the military and oil. In 1942, the Army Air Force Bombardier Training School, located near Midland, was the world's largest military training facility. Many of the school's cadets needed homes for their wives and children. In addition, many oil companies chose Midland as their home during the 1940s. This combination created a shortage of homes in Midland. Harold, whose father was a builder, realized that he had both the determination and the talent to help solve that problem. Harold worked as a district manager for CIT Credit Corporation, an institution that financed automobile dealerships. But he spent his spare time learning as much as he could about the building business. Eventually he learned so much about the industry that he was able to quit his job at CIT and form a business with a local contractor, even though he had no formal training. Jenna Welch helped keep the business running smoothly by acting as the company's bookkeeper. (Years later, her daughter would also play an important "behind-the-scenes" role to support her own husband's career.) When Laura was born, Jenna insisted on working from home so that she could take care of her only daughter.

Harold and Jenna built a loving home for Laura. In an interview with Oprah Winfrey for *O, The Oprah Magazine* in May 2001, Laura recalled, "I was lucky to have loving parents who made me feel secure, and that has been a huge advantage." The Welch home was a comfortable place for her childhood friends to spend time, also. Jan Donnelly O'Neill, the woman who introduced Laura to her future husband years later, says, "You always loved to hang out at their house. You just always laughed and had a good time . . . sitting down and having Cokes with Laura and her mom and dad."

Harold and Jenna Welch were Democrats, and their daughter continued that family tradition. Early in her relationship with George W. Bush, a staunch Republican, Laura would inform him that she was not very involved in politics and that she was a registered Democrat. But she did not tell him at the time that she had voted for antiwar candidate George McGovern for president in 1972. In casting that vote, she had voted against Richard Nixon, whom George's father, George Bush Sr., had supported.

Although Harold and Jenna Welch doted on their beloved daughter, they longed for more children. They suffered several miscarriages and stillbirths, and several premature babies died only a few days after birth. At one point, they even considered adoption. They took Laura with them to the adoption agency, but they finally decided not to follow through with the adoption proceedings. From a young age, Laura was sensitive to the pain that this caused her parents. Today Laura acknowledges that it is perhaps as a result of this that she felt additional pressure to be a good daughter. "I felt very obligated to my parents. I didn't want to upset them in any way. I just wanted to be the best little girl I could possibly be. I wanted them to be happy with our little family."

"The Best Little Girl"

In many ways, Laura was indeed "the best little girl." A childhood friend, Peggy Porter Weiss, recalls finding Laura removing several ticks from Marty, her dog. "I remember thinking, 'Oh my gosh, I would never do this, and if someone forced me to do this, I would complain the whole time.'" When Peggy expressed her disgust, Laura said casually, "It's not so bad!" Her mother remembers her as an easygoing, good-natured child. "She just never whined the way other kids do," Jenna says. "I know it sounds unbelievable, but it's hard to think of a time when she ever talked back or griped about having to do something." And, according to Jenna, that pleasant disposition is still evident today. "She is just eager to please—always has been," Jenna says. "She will do whatever is asked of her, and she'll do it without complaint."

In 1950, Laura attended kindergarten. By the end of her first week at school, she had memorized the first and last names of all the children in her class—there were more than 20 of them. She had even memorized the names of all the members of the teaching staff. She did the same for all the children she met at her swimming lessons, ballet lessons, and children's choir that year. (Her future husband would display a similar talent in college: He became the first pledge in the history of his fraternity to recite the names of all 50 of his fellow pledges.) Laura's mother points out that this early talent was useful in Laura's career. "When she was school librarian, she had 700 kids in the school, and she tried to remember the names of as many as she could," says Jenna Welch.

Laura's activities in her childhood, even at such a young age, helped to shape the woman she would eventually become. Choir practice, for example, taught her dedication, determination, and other traits that were important in her teaching career years later. "They sang in church [only] once or twice a year, but they went every week for choir practice," says Jenna. This, according to Jenna, also helped teach her daughter discipline. In addition, Laura's decision to continue with this pastime throughout primary school was even useful for her college career. "Laura sang in the choir until the eighth grade, and this training helped her when she got to college and studied the music courses that all education majors are required to take," Jenna adds.

Girl Scout

Another important influence in Laura's early years was her participation in the Girl Scouts of the USA. Once a week after school, Laura would attend a Brownie troop meeting with some of her friends. The troop's leaders, Mrs. Barrett and Mrs. Smith, tried to "mold a lively group of seven-year-olds into domestic young ladies," according to a daughter of one of the troop leaders. "Laura was one of my mom's favorites because she listened quietly and followed directions well," she adds.

Laura would later graduate from Brownies to Girl Scouts, through which she had many opportunities to enjoy nature and the outdoors. This gave her an appreciation for the outdoors that she still enjoys today. She and a group of her longtime friends have occasionally taken adventure trips, such as white-water rafting expeditions, as recently as their 55th birthdays.

In addition to playing those influential roles in Laura's life, the Girl Scouts of the USA helped Laura reach an important milestone in her life. As the only child of two adoring parents, Laura led a fairly sheltered childhood. When she graduated to the Junior Girl Scouts at the age of eight, Laura attended her first summer camp. The camp was in the Davis Mountains, about 200 miles away from her home in Midland. It was the longest she had ever been away from home. She stayed at the camp for only a week.

Then she called her parents and asked to go home. "I think she was homesick," Jenna says. "She wouldn't go back for a year or two." The next time she went to the camp, she was able to enjoy the experience. Realizing how much she had grown helped the shy young girl gain self-confidence. This confidence would surely help her later in life as a teacher.

The benefits Laura received from the Girl Scouts of America had a lasting effect on her. In fact, the organization benefited her in other ways when she was an adult. In a speech at the first Texas Book Festival in 1996, Laura noted a positive influence that the Girl Scouts of the USA has had on one of her favorite subjects: education. "Through a program called Experience Corps, retired senior citizens put their wisdom and experience to work, helping low-income children learn how to read. Boy Scouts and Girl Scouts took up the challenge, committing thousands of volunteer hours in one-on-one tutoring or group projects."

There were many other factors in Laura's early years that influenced the person she would eventually grow up to be. From an early age, Laura knew what she wanted to be when she grew up. "I first decided to become a teacher when I was in the second grade," she said in her speech at the 2000 Republican National Convention. Laura's decision was influenced by two important women in her life. One was her mother, who had taken her to the public library in Midland when she was very young. Another important influence was her second-grade teacher, Charlene Gnagy. In fact, during an interview for *Reader's Digest*, Laura said Mrs. Gnagy was the one person outside of her family who had been most influential in her life. "I wanted to be so much like her I decided in the second grade I wanted to teach," Laura said. When she was a young girl, one of her favorite games was playing teacher, using dolls as pupils. "Years later, our daughters did the same thing," Laura added. "We used to joke that the Bush family had the best educated dolls in America."

A Love of Reading

Laura's passion for books was evident early in her school years. In primary school, some of her favorite books were the *Little House* series by Laura Ingalls Wilder, the *Bobbsey Twins* series, *Little Women*, and *The Secret Garden*. Childhood friend Gwyne Smith Bohren recalls, "I wasn't a great reader back then, but Laura was *always* reading." Even the name she chose for one of her cats displayed Laura's love for books: She called the cat Dewey, after the Dewey Decimal System used in libraries.

Laura shared her love of reading with her mother. "She liked to cook, as all little girls do," Jenna Welch says. "She enjoyed making cookies, muffins, and things, and she's pretty good at casseroles. But the main interest we've always shared is books." In an interview with *People* magazine in 2001, Laura warmly recalled the role that reading played in her loving relationship with her mother. "Some of my fondest memories are of sitting with my mother's arms around me, listening to her read," she said. "Little did I know that she was doing much more than providing comfort and entertainment. She was paving the way for learning and for success." When she was a teenager, Laura would often read aloud to her mother during long drives together, with Jenna at the wheel. This tradition continued when Laura was old enough to drive; mother and daughter would take turns as driver and reader. In this way, Laura and her mother read several books to each other—including Laura's favorite, a famous and very complicated novel called *The Brothers Karamazov*, by Fyodor Dostoevsky.

But the book that probably had the most important influence on the course of her young life was *Doak Walker: Three-Time All-American*. This was the story of a legendary football player at Southern Methodist University (SMU), in Dallas. Walker said that the school had helped to shape his values. Laura read the story of Doak Walker when she was 12 years old. That's when she decided that she, too, wanted to attend Southern Methodist University. And as she expected, SMU would later be an important influence in her life.

A Friend to Everybody

Doak Walker, the legendary football player from Southern Methodist University, inspired Laura to attend that same university. (Associated Press)

Throughout her school years, Laura was well liked by her classmates and was a good student. In the late 1950s, Laura started attending San Jacinto Junior High School with many of the same friends she had known in grade school. Also in her class were students who had transferred from smaller, private schools. Laura was aware that these students probably felt uncomfortable being the new kids in school. Many of her classmates remember her as a sweet, friendly girl who went out of her way to make others feel welcome. The same year Laura entered San Jacinto, Cindy Schumann Klatt was a transfer student from a local private school, St. Ann's. "My first memory of Laura is how friendly and concerned she was that those of us from St. Ann's were included in the activities around school," she says. Karen Thompson Trout was another new arrival at San Jacinto Junior High.

"When I think of Laura and junior high, I think of what a sincere person she was, and how she treated people so nicely," she says. "She always was a friend to everybody." Even as a teenager, Laura was exhibiting traits that made her a natural teacher: She was very accepting and made people feel included rather than left out, and she made an effort to be friendly to everyone.

Laura continued to be very popular and very studious in high school. She worked on the yearbook, took honors classes, and was an A student. Many students who devote a lot of time to studying sometimes forget how important it is to have a satisfying social life. But Laura treasured her friends, and she always found time to socialize with them. She was popular with her female classmates, who cherished her friendship and enjoyed spending time with her. She was also well liked by her male classmates, and she dated often.

One Fateful Night . . .

One of the boys Laura dated during her junior year in high school was Michael D. Douglas. Mike was a track star and a member of the football team. Like Laura, he excelled at almost everything he tried, and he had many friends. In fact, in his junior year, he was nominated as the most popular boy in his school. Classmate Joe O'Neill says, "Mike was a superstar. He was a terrific athlete, a top student, great-looking, incredibly nice—everybody loved him."

Although their relationship had ended by their senior year, Mike and Laura remained friends. But Mike's role in Laura's life was not over. In fact, he would have a very significant impact on the way she viewed life for years to come.

On November 6, 1963, two days after her 17th birthday, Laura asked to borrow the family car. Knowing that their daughter was responsible, her parents quickly gave Laura the keys to their brand-new car. "Don't worry," Laura told her parents. "I promise I'll be home by ten."

Laura picked up her friend Judy Dykes and headed for a party. Traveling at 15 miles below the speed limit on Farm Road 868 as she chatted with her friend, Laura failed to notice a stop sign. She drove through the intersection without stopping, into the side of a car traveling on the intersecting road. Laura and Judy were immediately taken to the hospital. Fortunately, they suffered only a few scratches and bruises in the accident. The young man in the other car, however, was not as lucky. His neck had broken as soon as the Welches' car hit him, and he was dead.

Later that night, Laura learned the truth about the driver of the car she had hit: Not only had the young man died, but he was her friend Mike Douglas.

According to Robert McCleskey, a friend of both Laura and Mike, the residents of Midland did not blame Laura for the accident. Fortunately for Laura, Mike's parents showed her the same graciousness that she always showed to others throughout her life. "The Douglases were good people, kind people," McCleskey adds. "They were fond of Laura and knew it was just a freak accident—the kind of thing that could happen to anybody."

Nevertheless, Laura was devastated by the tragedy. She stayed home from school for a week after the accident, crying in her room for most of that time. When she found the strength to leave the house, it was usually only to speak with the pastor of her church, First United Methodist Church. Laura found comfort in the pastor's words as she tried to deal with the pain and grief of the tragic accident.

Only two weeks later, Laura's accident was overshadowed by an event in Texas that would have a serious impact on not just Midland but the entire world. John F. Kennedy, president of the United States, was shot and killed while visiting Dallas. Throughout the country, Americans were shocked by the news. And though she was still overcome with grief by her own recent tragedy, Laura later said that the assassination of JFK was "the most traumatic time in [her] childhood." When Laura returned to school, Robert McCleskey says, "She had a good circle of friends to support her. She didn't change in any way that I could tell." Many of Laura's friends, however, felt that she had been forever changed by her accident. "Just look in Laura's eyes. The pain is right there," said one of her friends. "Some of the spark was gone," a classmate said later. "She was still a pretty upbeat person, but it was just clear that some of the spontaneity and joy had gone out of her life."

Unfortunately for Laura, when her husband was campaigning as a presidential nominee for the Republican Party in 2000, the story of the accident was publicized across the country. In several interviews, she was forced to recall the ordeal. "I grieved a lot. It was a horrible, horrible accident," Laura said in an interview. Acknowledging the impact that the accident had had on her philosophy of life, she explained, "It was a sign of the preciousness of life and how fleeting it can be." And in an interview in 2001, Laura again confirmed the important life lesson that came out of that tragic night in 1963. "I truly think life is a gift," she said, "and everything in the world is a gift to all of us."

3

FROM COLLEGE STUDENT TO CAREER WOMAN

The year 1964 was an eventful one. Civil rights leader Martin Luther King Jr. was awarded the Nobel Peace Prize. The World's Fair opened in New York. North America's largest earthquake ever recorded occurred in Alaska. Ford produced its first Mustang. The Beatles appeared on *The Ed Sullivan Show*. And Laura Welch went off to college.

Laura entered Southern Methodist University in Dallas in the fall of that year. Choosing SMU was the first step toward fulfilling the dream she had had since she was 12 years old, when she was inspired by the story of SMU graduate Doak Walker. Choosing elementary education as her major was the first step toward fulfilling another dream, one she had had since she was seven years old: to become a teacher.

Although neither of Laura's parents had graduated from college, she knew at a young age that they expected her to go to college when she was old enough. "Don't worry, your college education will be taken care of," Harold Welch had told his daughter when she was very young.

Laura's decision to major in education was not unusual for a woman in those days. Today, women have an extensive variety of career choices. In the 1960s, however, they had very few options. Laura acknowledges that her career choice was a traditional but nevertheless important one. "When I describe myself as traditional, I mean in the sense that I had jobs that were traditionally women's jobs. But I never felt I was so traditional," she said years later about her career choices. "For instance, teaching in minority schools, you know, not marrying until my thirties. I felt I was in many ways very contemporary."

College Days

The 1960s were very turbulent. Many people, especially those of college age, wanted political change. They wanted people to have more freedom, and they didn't want the United States to be involved in a war against Vietnam. They were struggling for peace, but along with their actions came what many people considered a change in morals. In other words, people's ideas about good behavior were being challenged.

This environment was especially evident on college campuses. Southern Methodist University, however, was different. It was one of the most conservative colleges in the country at that time. Most of the teachers and students there felt that traditional values were still important. They were more protected from the chaos related to the call for political change. So, just as Midland protected Laura in her hometown, her college sheltered her from the outside world when she was away from home.

Laura was an A student in college, just as she had been throughout her school career. She studied hard and didn't "party" like students of many other colleges in the 1960s. But she still found time to have fun. In fact, according to sorority sister Susan Nowlin, "Her room was always the central headquarters for fun." For enjoyment, Laura and her friends went to the pool, drank soda, played cards, listened to records, and smoked cigarettes. (Laura eventually quit smoking, but she had started smoking before people knew that it was harmful to them.) She joined a sorority called Kappa Alpha Theta, and she had many friends. She also had many male admirers, but according to a longtime friend, "She would never allow herself to get serious about anyone. She kept every boy who showed signs of wanting something more at arm's length."

A Moment of Doubt

In 1968, Laura graduated from SMU with a bachelor's degree in education. The school would always hold a very special place in her life, long after she became first lady of Texas and then of the United States. About 30 years after Laura graduated from Southern Methodist University, the college awarded her a Distinguished Alumni award. It was SMU's way of thanking her for her work to support libraries, literacy, and childhood education. That same year, SMU dedicated the Laura Bush Promenade, a garden walkway into one of the school's many libraries. Laura's husband was the governor of Texas at that time. George W. Bush had given SMU $250,000 to build the promenade. Laura later said the promenade was "the nicest and most romantic gift" she had ever received from her husband. "And when I opened the gifts under the Christmas tree that year, there was a little porcelain copy of the Fondren Library Center, the library at SMU, and then a drawing of the garden promenade," she added. In addition, seven of the First Lady's Kappa Alpha Theta sorority sisters from SMU honored her by giving funds to the library as a tribute to their friendship.

The Wayfaring Welches

After graduation from SMU, Laura was eager to begin her teaching career. But she told her parents that she wanted to go backpacking through Europe with her friends before she started working. Harold and Jenna Welch were concerned. Luckily for Laura and her parents, her uncle, a surgeon, had an idea that made all of them happy.

"Originally Laura told us that she wanted to go with a group of college girls on a European camping trip, but we weren't too sure about that; we were pretty protective," Jenna says. "But then this chance came along and she wanted to go."

Laura and her husband, then Governor George W. Bush, at the ceremony where Laura received the Distinguished Alumni award from Southern Methodist University (Associated Press)

The idea was that Laura would accompany her aunt, uncle, and cousin to Europe. Dr. Mark Welch had already booked a two-week medical conference to several countries in Europe, and he invited Laura to join his family on the trip. "It was a magical experience," Laura told her mother later. "It made all the things I'd read about in books come alive."

Laura knew that as soon as she returned from Europe, she would want to start working. So before she left, she applied for a job with the Dallas Public School system.

When she returned from her trip, however, she found out that there were no jobs available in Dallas schools. Laura was disappointed, but she wasn't discouraged. In the meantime, she accepted a clerical position at an insurance company in Dallas. A couple of months later, Laura was offered a job as a third-grade teacher in Dallas. She accepted the position eagerly.

Miss Welch the Teacher

When Laura started teaching her first class, she was shocked. Her students were eight and nine years old, but many of them could not read. She tried to think of new ways to help her students to learn and enjoy reading. "I tried to make it fun by making the characters in children's books members of our class," she says. Referring to the second-grade teacher who inspired her to become a teacher, Laura says, "After working as a teacher in Dallas, I gained a whole new respect for Mrs. Gnagy. But I loved every minute of it." Although she enjoyed teaching in Dallas, the experience made Laura realize that teachers "need better training in what works to teach children to read."

About her early years as a teacher, Laura says, "A love of reading does not automatically translate into the ability to teach a child to read. Even with a degree in education and practice as a student teacher, I wasn't totally prepared for teaching reading. I took pride in my educational training, but the job was much harder than I had imagined." Years later, never forgetting the important lesson she learned, Laura would work hard to support teacher-training programs.

After a year in Dallas, Laura started teaching second grade at John F. Kennedy Elementary School in a Houston neighborhood. Most of the residents of the neighborhood were African American. Working in the Houston neighborhood was an eye-opening experience for Laura—maybe because she had led a fairly sheltered life even throughout her college years. "I particularly wanted to work in a minority school," she says. Of her students, she says, "I'm sure I learned more from them than they did from me—most importantly, I think, about the dignity of every human child."

Laura adored her students, and they liked having her for their teacher. She knew how important it was for her as a teacher to have a good relationship with her students. "There aren't many jobs where hero and best friend are part of the job description," she said years later. Laura liked the students in her first class at John F. Kennedy so much that at the end of the school year, she asked to teach the same students in third grade the next year.

A Teacher Goes Back to School

Laura taught at JFK Elementary School for two years. In 1970, she began to attend courses at the University of

Texas in Austin. She intended to get a master's degree in library science and become a librarian.

Laura took classes at the University of Texas for two years. The classes she took prepared her for the most basic functions of a librarian. She learned how to categorize books in a logical order, and she learned about the history of libraries. More important, she found ways to expand her talents as a teacher of reading. She learned how to figure out if certain books are appropriate for children. She was taught techniques to help children understand the concept of reading. And she learned how to help children enjoy reading as much she did.

Laura graduated with a master of library science degree in 1973. She is only the second first lady to have a graduate degree. (Hillary Rodham Clinton, who holds a law degree, was the first.)

Laura started working as a librarian the year after she graduated from the University of Texas. Her first job as a librarian was in Houston, the same city where she had so loved teaching the children at John F. Kennedy Elementary School. She moved to Houston and worked as a children's librarian at a public library.

Laura stayed in Houston for a year before moving back to Austin, where she took a job as librarian at Mollie Dawson Elementary School. She was very happy to be both working as a librarian and working with elementary

From College Student to Career Woman • 27

Ever since her days as a librarian in Texas, Laura has been a champion of libraries and literacy. (Landov)

school children. Most of the students at Dawson Elementary School were Hispanic. Laura again enjoyed working with these children from backgrounds different from hers. "I think teaching in minority schools opened my eyes," she says. "It made me realize how unfair in a lot of ways life is."

Laura was dedicated to her career, but as always she did not forget the importance of friendship. Her friends say that she did not seem concerned that she was single while most of them were getting married. Regan Gammon, one of her closest friends, says, "I never once heard her say, 'I wish I could find someone I wanted to marry.'"

Laura continued to work as a children's librarian in Austin until 1977, the year she would meet George W. Bush and her life would be changed forever.

4

MARRIAGE AND FAMILY

Before they were formally introduced, Laura Welch and George W. Bush had probably crossed paths several times without realizing it. After all, when they were children, their families lived in the same part of town in Midland, Texas. One year, they attended the same middle school. For a time after college, they lived in the same apartment complex. When they were in their 20s, George worked for a program that helped some of the same inner-city children whom Laura knew from her job as a librarian in the same town. And they were even friends with some of the same people. But it was the active efforts of two friends that ultimately brought them together.

Opposites Attract

In 1977, most of Laura Welch's friends were married, and many of them already had children. But not Laura. She was working as a librarian at Mollie Dawson Elementary School in Austin, Texas. According to her friends, Laura was content with her career and did not feel pressured to get married right away.

Many of her friends, however, felt differently. They knew the librarian and teacher would also make a wonderful wife and mother. Laura later joked about her friends' efforts to get her to meet George W. Bush. "I think all of our friends wanted to fix us up because we were literally the last two who hadn't married of all of our friends." Laura's friend Jan Donnelly was one of the friends who hoped Laura would get married. Jan had married George's childhood friend Joe O'Neill in 1972, and Jan and Joe hoped that George and Laura would hit it off. But even the friends who wanted to fix them up were not sure the two would get along, as they had very different personalities.

In spite of their doubts, Jan and Joe worked together to try to get Laura Welch the librarian to meet George W. Bush the oil businessman. But Laura was hesitant for several reasons. One problem for her was that George lived in Midland, which was a five-hour car ride from where she worked in Austin. When Laura did make the drive from Austin to Midland on weekends, she wanted to spend time with her family. Also, George came from a family of politicians. In July 1977, he announced that he was running for a seat in Congress. Laura, on the other hand, was not involved in politics. "I was just so uninterested in politics," she says. "I thought he was someone [really] political, and I wasn't interested." In fact, George would say later, "She really didn't care for politicians."

But one night in August 1977, Laura finally agreed to meet George at a cookout at the O'Neills' home. Their friends were pleasantly surprised at how quickly George and Laura hit it off that night. "I don't know that it was love at first sight," Laura would say later, "but it was close." George was attracted to Laura immediately. He says he saw a woman who "turned out [to be not only] elegant and beautiful, but very smart."

Laura told her mother later that night, "The thing I like about him is that he made me laugh." She later explained, "I liked that he gave me a lot of energy because of the energy of his personality. Plus, he was funny and we laughed a lot. Both of us love to laugh, and I think that's great."

Usually, George left evening gatherings by nine o'clock. He normally woke up at around six o'clock each morning to run three miles. But that night, George stayed at the party until midnight, talking and laughing with Laura. "I found her to be a very thoughtful, smart, interested person—one of the great listeners," George says about Laura. "And since I'm one of the great talkers, it was a great fit." Most of their friends and family agree with George's assessment: The two have many more differences than similarities. She is so neat and organized that she arranges the family's books according to the Dewey Decimal System; he is much less orderly. She is modest and humble, while George is outspoken and arrogant at times. With the exception of her short courtship with George before agreeing to marry him, she is known to think before acting; he tends to be impulsive and spontaneous. And of course, Laura is quiet and conservative, while George is talkative and is known for having a wild side.

The night they met, George told Laura that he wanted to see her again. Both of them knew that the distance between Austin and Midland might make it difficult for them to have a serious relationship. Nonetheless, they decided to make an effort. George, Laura, Joe, and Jan played miniature golf together the very next night. The next weekend, instead of Laura driving to Midland to see her family, George drove to Austin to see her. The next day, George flew to Maine for the Bush family's vacation, but he couldn't stay away from Laura for long; after just one day in Maine, he flew back to Austin to see her. Over the next few weeks, George flew to Austin from Midland as often as he could so that he could continue to spend time with her. They became very close very quickly. "It was almost like we'd known each other forever," Laura recalls. "We had so much of the same background."

Laura was facing her 31st birthday at the time, and today she acknowledges that it might have been an important reason that she and George seemed to be moving their relationship along so quickly. "I'm sure both of us thought, 'Gosh, we may never get married.' And we both really wanted children." In addition, Laura points out that it was difficult for them to spend time together when they lived so far away from each other. If they were married, they would be living in the same home.

Laura and George had known each other only three weeks when George proposed marriage to Laura, and they had known each other only three months when they were married in November of 1977. They did not have time to plan a lavish wedding, but they admit that they did not want an elaborate celebration anyway. So, like the bride herself, the wedding ceremony was simple and unpretentious—not showy at all. It was attended by only 75 guests, a fraction of the two popular families' friends and relatives. There were no bridesmaids or groomsmen. The invitations had been handwritten by the mother of the bride rather than professionally printed. And Laura wore a simple cream-colored dress rather than a fancy white bridal gown. "No fuss," says George W. Bush. "We just wanted to get married, and we wanted our closest friends and families there to celebrate with us."

George and Laura on their wedding day with George's parents, Barbara and George Bush (Associated Press/White House)

The ceremony took place November 5, 1977, at the First United Methodist Church in Midland. "It was in the church I'd been baptized in as a baby and had always gone to and in the church that George joined with me and where our babies were [later] baptized," Laura says. "So it was a really wonderful way to start a new marriage."

Hitting the Campaign Trail

Although their opposite personalities attracted George and Laura to each other, the newlyweds knew that it would take a while to get used to living in the same home. They did not have much time to adjust, however. After a short honeymoon in Mexico, Laura moved into George's large brick house on Golf Course Road in Midland. George had bought the house for $200,000 earlier that year—a large sum for a house in 1976. But soon after the marriage, George W. Bush began his first political campaign for Congress. Although Laura had always considered herself a Democrat ("I'm a Republican by marriage," she says), she was prepared to help her husband's campaign efforts. Doing so would mean devoting a lot of her time—and giving up her beloved job as a librarian.

George and Laura spent their first year of marriage campaigning. Laura worried about the strain it would place on their relationship. After all, they were still getting to know each other when they hit the campaign trail. But campaigning together turned out to be an advantage for them. As George explains: "We were united on a common mission; we spent lots of time together." And Laura did indeed have the opportunity to learn more about her new husband during the campaign. She was surprised to see how well he connected with voters. "George was great," she says of her husband. "I always thought he said the right thing."

Because Laura was a newcomer to politics, especially being the wife of a political candidate, she had asked her mother-in-law, Barbara Bush, for advice. As George Sr.'s wife, Barbara had a lot of experience with being married to a politician. She gave Laura some guidance about how to behave and then said seriously, "Don't ever, ever criticize your husband's speeches."

One night, toward the end of his campaign, George did not feel confident about the speech he had given in Lubbock earlier that day. During the long car ride home,

Laura hit the campaign trail for George's run for Congress not long after the two were married. (George Bush Presidential Library)

he hoped Laura would say something encouraging about his speech. But she had been careful to follow Barbara's advice not to say anything negative about her husband's speeches, and she was determined not to start now. Instead of being dishonest, she said nothing. As George pulled the car into the driveway, he asked Laura directly, "I didn't do very well, did I?" "No, it wasn't very good," Laura finally agreed. George was so surprised that he drove into the garage wall.

George eventually lost the campaign to his Democratic opponent, Texas State Senator Kent Hance. Although Hance became one of George's supporters years later, the defeat gave George a taste of how dirty politics can be. "It was my first confrontation with cheap-shot politics," he says. He and Laura were extremely disappointed by the loss. The defeat had some positive effects, however. For one thing, Laura had practiced and improved her public-speaking skills, which she would certainly need in the future. In addition, many Texans felt that the experience made George humbler and less arrogant.

From Trail to Field

A defeat at the polls wasn't the only thing that would help to make George humbler. Another factor was his defeat in the oil fields. After the election, George and Laura returned to their home in Midland, and George returned to his oil business. Several investors, many of whom were friends of the Bush family, gave George money to drill for oil. If he found oil, both George and the investors would profit. But time after time, George dug up a dry hole. He then had to call his investors and admit that he had lost their money; he had again been defeated. And with each call admitting that he had lost, perhaps a little of George's pride was lost also.

Around the time that George was working to build up his oil business, his father, George Herbert Walker Bush, failed to be nominated as the Republican candidate for president. Instead, the Republicans nominated Ronald Reagan as their candidate to run against the current president, Jimmy Carter. George Sr. became Ronald Reagan's running mate, and in January 1981, he was sworn in as the first Bush to serve as vice president of the United States. Only two months later, there was an assassination attempt on President Reagan's life. George and Laura watched the news coverage and waited to hear whether the president would recover. As they waited, they wondered whether a horrible tragedy such as this would put the first Bush in the White House. Fortunately, Ronald Reagan recovered quickly and completely—so completely, in fact, that the Reagan-Bush team would later be reelected to serve in the White House, from 1986 to 1989.

Despite the frustration of George's struggling oil business, George and Laura realized that his campaign loss had one additional benefit: The defeat also gave them the opportunity to do what the campaign had forced them to postpone. It was time for them to settle into their home and start living like a typical married family.

Family Life

Unlike George, Laura did not return to the job she had held before she and George got married. Always able to adapt to change, Laura easily filled the role of homemaker. She enjoyed keeping the house clean and the garden beautiful. She also became involved in community activities. Laura volunteered for Midland's chapter of the Junior League, a women's organization that works to make communities healthier. The Junior League promotes important issues for women and children, such as women's shelters, protection from diseases, and a matter that would become one of Laura's favorite topics of speeches: literacy.

Laura was content as a homemaker, and George was hard at work developing his oil business. But they both still wanted to have children. Although doctors told Laura she would probably never be able to bear a child, she and George were determined to build a family. So, in the spring of 1981, they drove to the Gladney adoption home in Forth Worth. It was the same adoption home that Laura's parents had visited in the hopes of adopting a child before they changed their minds. It was also the home from which three couples who were among their closest friends had adopted children. George and Laura had already taken several steps in the adoption process when they got a shock: Laura was pregnant.

George and Laura were thrilled about her pregnancy, but there was more news. One day in the doctor's office, the Bushes learned that Laura was carrying twins. Husband and wife immediately broke down in tears of joy. George, always supportive, was determined that Laura's pregnancy would be a pleasant time for her. The day after hearing the news, he sent her two dozen red roses with a card that read, "From the father of twins."

While George and Laura were delighted to be having twins, carrying two babies made Laura's pregnancy even more dangerous for her. She had to be very careful, and she had to relax as much as possible throughout her pregnancy. In her sixth month of pregnancy, she developed a dangerous condition called toxemia, which threatened the lives of Laura and her babies. Laura's doctor told her that she would be lucky to deliver one healthy child. But George and Laura had waited too long for their dream to come true, so they did everything they could to keep their babies safe. Laura stayed home rather than join George for his family's vacation to Maine. And, just as when they first met, George could not stay away from Laura; he flew back to Midland the next day to be with her. By September, Laura's doctors were urging her to deliver her babies as soon as possible. Waiting any longer could be even more dangerous for Laura.

But Laura knew that waiting longer would give her babies more time to grow stronger and healthier before being born. "These babies are going to be born healthy," she told her husband. "They're going to stay with me until they're big enough." So she insisted on waiting as long as possible.

George has marveled at his wife's strength and bravery during that time. "She was heroic," he says. "There was an unbelievable will to protect the children." He says that Laura's determination inspired him. "I remember to this day how confident I became because of her."

Laura waited as long as she could, until doctors warned her that her kidneys might stop working. So, on November 25, 1981—five weeks before her due date—Laura gave birth to twin girls. The girls were named after their grandmothers: Barbara and Jenna. "I was in the operating room," George says about the birth of their daughters. "I'm an emotional person. I got weepy, and then I realized our life had changed forever, in a positive way." He admires Laura's willingness to risk her own safety for the sake of her children. "She loves our daughters more than anything," he says. "She would lay her life down for them, and nearly did at [their] birth."

After more than a decade of looking after other people's children, it was time for Laura to turn her attention toward her own two daughters. But as Laura points out, "Babies don't come with sets of instructions." So for the first few months, she and George paid a part-time nurse to help them. Soon the girls were following a routine, and the new mom and dad were caring for their daughters themselves. Laura's parents lived eight blocks away, and her father visited almost every day. George and Laura also brought the girls to visit Harold and Jenna Welch almost every day. When George arrived home late from work, he would often find Laura working in the garden after the twins had been tucked into bed for the night. If the girls were still awake when he got home, he would entertain them by tickling them, rolling around with them on the living room floor, making funny faces at them,

The Bush family (George Bush Presidential Library)

or reading to them. "George and I always read to our girls—Dr. Seuss's *Hop on Pop* was one of his favorites," Laura said in a speech. "George would lie on the floor and the girls would literally hop on pop, turning story time into a contact sport." George and Laura wanted their daughters to enjoy reading. "We wanted to teach our children what our parents had taught us . . . that reading is entertaining and interesting and important," she said.

And it seems that the Bush twins understood their parents' message about the importance of literacy and education. Jenna would graduate from the University of Texas at Austin in the spring of 2004 with plans to be a teacher, while Barbara, like their father, grandfather, and great-grandfather, would graduate from Yale University in New Haven, Connecticut.

Ups and Downs

George and Laura were thrilled with their new life together, but they went through good times and bad times in the first 16 years of their marriage. With his work in the oil business, George suffered some financial losses followed by business dealings that were much more profitable. But he had almost lost something much more serious than money. George often had an alcoholic beverage when he got home from work. When business was not going well, his casual drinking became more frequent and more serious. Laura told him that he had to choose between his alcohol and his family. In 1986, he realized that giving up his drinking habit was a small price to pay to keep his wife and daughters. In giving a reason for his decision to quit, George says, "The best explanation is to say that alcohol was beginning to compete for my affections—compete for my affections with my wife and family." He adds, "It was beginning to crowd out my energy, and I decided to quit."

Another challenge that the family faced was a huge move in 1987—from the comfort of their home in Midland to the unfamiliar and very different world of Washington, D.C. George Sr., serving his second term as vice president under Ronald Reagan, had decided to run for president, and George wanted to help. Laura was content in the traditional roles of housewife and mother. She was participating in the Parent Teacher Organization of her daughters' school, volunteering at the school library, and enjoying her life with other housewives and mothers in the neighborhood. Life, Laura says, seemed "awfully close to perfect." So while she was reluctant to make the move, Laura knew how much George wanted to help his father in his campaign for president. She agreed.

A New Home in Dallas

George Sr., with Dan Quayle as his running mate, was successful in his campaign to be the 41st president of the

United States. In 1989, George, Laura, and their daughters soon moved back to Texas—this time to Dallas. There, George became managing general partner of the Texas Rangers Major League Baseball franchise. At the time, the Texas Rangers were playing in a run-down, outdated ballpark; this gave George a chance to make a mark. As a managing general partner, George helped to create a beautiful new stadium with special features such as a restaurant, a children's center, a museum, and offices. The facility was more enjoyable for the fans and more profitable for the stadium. Another advantage of the business arrangement was that it became a family tradition for the Bushes. George and Laura attended four or five dozen Rangers games per season for five years in a row. When the twins were not at summer camp, they often joined their parents at the games. But for George, one of the most important benefits of the Texas Rangers deal was probably that he had been successful in business on his own, without any help from a member of his family. When he sold the team in 1998, he received almost $15 million—more than 20 times what he had initially invested in the team.

In 1989, local Republican candidates asked George to run for governor of Texas. Laura discouraged him from running. She was concerned that he would lose and that the timing wasn't right. Following her advice, he declined, saying, "For now, I want to focus on my job as managing general partner of the Texas Rangers and more importantly as a good father and good husband."

Then, in 1992, George Bush Sr. lost a presidential reelection campaign to Governor Bill Clinton of Arkansas. Throughout the campaign, George felt that the media were being overly liberal and unfair toward his father and even toward the rest of the family. Laura remembered this as a time when she least liked being a member of a political family. She recalls not wanting to read the newspaper during that campaign, sure that something negative was going to be said about her father-in-law or a member of his family. "It really hurts to see someone you love attacked," she says. "It gets to you after a while."

So the family had already experienced several ups and downs by 1993. But George, Laura, and the twins were about to face some additional challenges.

5
FIRST LADY OF TEXAS

In 1993, George had to make an important decision that would affect his family as much as it would affect him. He needed to decide whether he wanted to be the governor of Texas.

Republican politicians in Texas wanted George to run against Ann Richards, a Democrat who was the well-liked governor of Texas. Laura was worried that George might run for the wrong reasons. She thought he might have felt extra pressure because of the success of his grandfather, former U.S. Senator Prescott Sheldon Bush, and his father, the recent president. "Is running for governor something you want to do, or is it something you're doing because people are pushing you to do it?" she asked George, whom she affectionately called "Bushie." George explained later, "She wanted to make sure I wasn't running because I had something to prove."

In addition, George and Laura knew that political campaigns can be rough and that the family might be attacked in the newspapers and on TV. They had witnessed this firsthand with George W.'s campaign for Congress during their first year of marriage and with George Sr.'s presidential campaigns more recently. When asked years later about the worst part of being in a political family, Laura replied, "I think the criticism that you hear, I mean, just because that's a fact of life in politics. I think that's by far the hardest part." George and Laura knew that campaigning might be difficult for the family, and it was important to them to see the family happy.

On the Road Again

So it was a tough choice to make, but George eventually decided that he would indeed seek to be the governor of Texas. And as George and Laura had feared, the campaign was a dirty one. Ann Richards attacked George personally. She told voters that George "doesn't have a clue." She also tried to make voters believe that George was not qualified on his own but was taking advantage of his father's fame. George denied those accusations, pointing out his devotion to his family. "I'm not running because I'm George Bush's son; I'm running because I'm Barbara and Jenna's dad," he said.

George was hurt and angry about the personal attacks. But Laura told him it was important for him not to insult

Ann Richards in return. "They're just trying to get to you, Bushie," she told him. "Don't let them." If he ignored the comments, Ann Richards would look silly to voters. If he attacked her to defend himself, he would look silly too. Laura's opinion was very important to George at that time, and it still is now. "She is a very wise person, and when she talks, I pay close attention to what she has to say," George says.

Laura was able to convince George that just laughing along with his opponent rather than launching a counterattack was the best way to go. It was not the first time that she had kept his emotions in check, and it would not be the last. "Laura does have a very calming effect on people," Jenna Welch says. "I guess you have to be in control if you're a teacher and you've got to get a bunch of schoolchildren to behave." George also acknowledges that his wife helps him stay calm. "She is calm and she is steady," George says. "She's got great values and a huge heart."

Laura was less involved in her husband's campaign to be governor than she had been in his 1977 campaign for Congress. Still, she took part in campaign activities. At Republican Women's Clubs, she gave speeches about ways George planned to improve schools. She was no longer a teacher in a classroom, yet she wanted to find ways to promote better education for children.

During this time, Laura was given some sad news. Her father had Alzheimer's disease, and he was getting sicker very quickly. Alzheimer's disease affects the brain, causing memory loss and dementia. It can be very painful for someone to watch a loved one suffer from Alzheimer's. A friend of Laura's, familiar with her courage and her desire to never complain, says, "Laura was under a lot of stress, but of course she'd never let you see it." Laura stayed close to her parents' home whenever possible, instead of campaigning heavily.

George, on the other hand, spent long days on the road. But after traveling to a variety of locations throughout the huge state of Texas each day, he would return home to his wife and daughters rather than stay in a hotel without them.

Ann Richards had been very popular with the people of Texas during her term as governor, and she was favored to win. But George surprised the country by defeating her. The Bush family moved into the Governor's Mansion in Austin, the capital of Texas, in January 1995.

Shortly after George's victory was announced, Laura suddenly realized that being the "first family of Texas"—the family of the governor—would mean a very different life for her husband, her daughters, and herself. "I'm not sure I can handle this," she told George. "And the girls—they have a right to lead a normal life." Later, George explained that he understood his wife's concerns about moving to Austin. "She was a little fearful, maybe, about whether any of this life would be to her liking."

A New Home, a New Role

Somehow, Laura's ability to adapt to change helped her slip easily into the role of first lady of Texas. She decorated the living quarters of the Governor's Mansion to reflect her personal taste. This made the huge mansion seem a little more like home for the family. On the walls hung two works of art by John Clem Clarke, who had married a friend of Laura's from Southern Methodist University. Painted ceramic bean pots from Mexico adorned the bookshelves. And representing their opposite personalities, George's office was decorated quite differently from the area of the mansion that Laura had decorated. Displayed in his office was a valuable collection of 250 baseballs signed by professional baseball players. On one wall hung a portrait of Sam Houston, a former governor and military hero of Texas. Linking the portrait with the baseball collection, perhaps, was the fact that George's childhood school, Sam Houston Elementary School, was where his passion for baseball had begun.

The family adjusted to their new life in the Governor's Mansion by keeping their daily routine similar to the way it was before. They would wake up at six o'clock, and

The Texas Governor's Mansion served as Laura's home for five years. (Austin Convention and Visitors Bureau)

George would go downstairs to feed the family pets—at that time, the dog, Spot, and the cats, Willie and Cowboy. Then George would return to Laura with coffee and the day's newspapers. At eight o'clock, George would begin his workday at the capitol building across the street from the Governor's Mansion. He would be in a series of meetings for the next few hours until it was time for his daily run at the University of Texas. Then he would return to the Governor's Mansion for lunch with Laura, sometimes followed by an additional break to relax. Then he had more meetings until his workday ended at three o'clock.

After spending family time together in the evenings when possible, George and Laura would read in bed until they fell asleep; George's bedtime, as it had been when they first met, was still nine o'clock.

Literacy Advocate

Laura soon realized that there were advantages to living in the Governor's Mansion. After all, being the wife of the governor would allow her to voice her opinions on issues that were important to her. "If I'm going to be a public figure, I might as well do what I've always liked doing—which means acting like a librarian and getting people interested in reading." She became more involved in her role as first lady than she had probably expected. Her days were often filled with luncheons, ribbon-cutting ceremonies, committee hearings, and fundraising events. Once, when a reporter asked her if she had lost herself in all the activities involved with being the wife of the governor, she replied, "I haven't lost myself; I've found myself."

"I don't think Laura ever anticipated her life would turn out this way," George would say later. "But when she got out there, started giving speeches . . . she realized people listened to her."

Though she thinks of herself as "generally reserved and shy," Laura says she discovered a trick to make her feel more comfortable when she gives speeches. She imagines she is a librarian again, reading to children. "I wouldn't have thought of this before I started giving speeches, but reading over the top of a book like I did millions of times as a children's librarian is great practice."

Laura worked to promote many important causes during her tenure as first lady of Texas. As a former teacher and librarian, Laura had always made literacy a priority. As first lady of Texas, she worked to create programs that would improve literacy throughout the state. "Reading is to the mind what food is to the body," she said in a speech in 1996. "In Texas, nothing will take higher priority." The key to encouraging literacy, she says, is to "break the cycle of illiteracy"—to make sure adults are literate so that they can read to children and teach them to read, also. "Just as children should be reading more, so should entire families," she says.

Promoting literacy was a cause that Laura shared with her mother-in-law. Barbara Bush had helped to develop a national program for literacy when she was first lady of the United States. She joined Laura's efforts to promote literacy in Texas. And as Laura points out, Barbara Bush is usually successful when she sets a goal. "My mother-in-law got involved," Laura says, "and you know what happens when Barbara Bush gets involved in something."

Laura managed to get both Democrats and Republicans involved in her literacy efforts. (While most politicians are supported only by members of their own political party, Laura worked to include everyone, as is natural for her to do.) The group that Laura organized created a huge $215 million fund to promote a program called the First Lady's Family Literacy Initiative. The initiative created laws to encourage early childhood reading. The project distributed almost $1 million for programs encouraging parents to read with their children. An important part of the Family Literacy Initiative is the Experience Corps.

Promoting literacy is something Laura shares with her mother-in-law, former first lady Barbara Bush. (Getty Images)

Through this program, retired senior citizens help teach underprivileged children to read. The Ready to Read, Ready to Learn program was another initiative under the Family Literacy Program. Laura began that program during her term as first lady of Texas, but it would later become one of her pet projects during her time as first lady of the United States.

A Patron of the Arts

Laura is an art lover, and George eventually shared her interest in art. So promoting local artists was another of her goals as first lady of Texas. Adair Margo, a friend of the Bushes and the owner of a Texas art gallery, explains, "Their taste is less formal and more articulate, and they have a real taste for Latino and Mexican art." Tom Lea, an artist in El Paso, Texas, became one of George and Laura's favorite artists. The artist became more popular after George and Laura began to display some of his paintings in the Governor's Mansion and the capitol building. Laura chose paintings from several Texas artists each year to decorate her office in the Governor's Mansion. She also selected a local artist to illustrate the first family's Christmas cards each year.

In addition to paintings and illustrations, Laura enjoys sculpture. One of her exhibits in the capitol building included the works of Mary Page Huey, a sculptor from

Austin. She also added art treasures from throughout the state to the capitol collection, with the help of the Texas Capitol Historical Art Committee.

Laura's support of literacy and other issues would continue after her time as first lady of Texas. However, one stage of her life ended just three months after she and her family moved into the Governor's Mansion. Laura's father, Harold Welch, died of Alzheimer's disease at the age of 82. "He was a gentle, decent man," George says of Harold Welch. "He didn't have a mean bone in his body."

A Calming Influence

Long before George and Laura became governor and first lady of Texas, friends and family had been wondering how the two made their relationship work. It could be said that they followed the example of two people who are very close to them: Laura's parents.

"George's and Laura's fathers were very much alike—very outgoing, very funny," Jenna Welch says. She added that she assumed that was "part of the appeal" for Laura, who was very close with her father. Family friend Robert McCleskey agrees. "[Jenna] Welch was the quiet Sunday School teacher; Harold was the fun-loving type of guy who talked up a storm," he says. Laura, too, recognizes the similarities between her husband and her father. "Both my dad and George tried to make people feel good," she says.

Even today, many insist that Laura's ability to keep George humble, in addition to her calming influence on him, helps to keep their marriage together. Some people noticed it right away, but most agree that it became more evident—and more important—as years passed.

Many consider George to be a man who insists on having his own ideas and opinions. But he himself admits about Laura, "She influences me on . . . every matter of life, whether it be political issues, policy issues. She's got enormous influence on me." He appreciates her calm effect on him and acknowledges that her lack of interest in being political brings balance to his life. "As a man who goes about a hundred miles an hour, I find that attractive," he says. "Politics doesn't totally consume her, and as a result, it doesn't totally consume me."

Robert McCleskey points out Laura's ability to keep George's arrogance in check. "Laura can be plenty tough, and she can chew him out," he says. "I saw him once when he was giving orders to all these people and rattling off commands, and she just looked at him and said, 'Bushie, you're not president yet!'"

Family friend Joe O'Neill might admit that he had doubts when he and his wife initially fixed George and Laura up in 1977. But after seeing their relationship work, he says, "Once you find the right person, that part of the equation is done and you can get on with the other things." Acknowledging that Laura supports George but does not control him, Joe adds, "There's no burning ambition there. She's not pushing George from the back, but she truly changed him."

Laura's influence on George is sometimes as calm and quiet as she is herself. That does not make it less important, however. Eventually, her subtle, calming effect would be a powerful influence that George—and perhaps an entire nation—would soon rely on in the face of crisis.

Reelection

By 1998, rumors were circulating that George W. Bush, governor of Texas, wanted to be George W. Bush, president of the United States. That summer, polls showed that George was favored to be the Republican presidential candidate. Polls also predicted that he could even beat the Democratic candidate, Vice President Al Gore.

George would have to consider his family's needs before he could consider running for president. He asked Laura how she would feel about it. "Are you sure, Bushie?" she asked him. She reminded him about the misery that the family had experienced during George Sr.'s presidential reelection campaign in 1992. George and Laura's main concern was the welfare of their daughters. George himself had been the son of a president—but not, as he pointed out, at the age of 18. As 18-year-olds facing their first year at college, Jenna and Barbara would want their lives to remain private. But as daughters of the president, they knew they would be public figures. They had gotten a taste of that when their grandfather was president. So whenever George mentioned the idea of running for president, his daughters begged him not to.

Despite the encouraging polls in the summer of 1998, George Sr. warned his son that if he wanted to win the Republican nomination for president, he would have to win reelection as governor first. So later that year, George focused on his reelection campaign. In order to serve a second term as governor, he would have to defeat Texas land commissioner Gary Mauro. During his campaign for reelection as governor in 1998, he said, "There are many reasons I want people to reelect me as governor of Texas. The most important one may be to keep Laura Bush as first lady."

On November 4, 1998, George was reelected by a landslide. The victory made him the first governor in Texas history to be reelected to a consecutive four-year term. That day was historic for another reason: George's younger brother, Jeb, had been elected governor of Florida. The next step for the Bush family depended on George's decision whether to seek an even bigger office: president of the United States.

6

FIRST LADY OF THE UNITED STATES

If George were to become president—or even if he were to run and be defeated—the entire Bush family would be affected. So George and Laura decided that what their daughters wanted, not just what they themselves wanted, was an important factor in their decision.

A Family Decision

Jenna and Barbara had already made their feelings clear months before. George claims they "cried and cried" when he mentioned the possibility that he would run for president. They feared that they would have no privacy as the children of the president of the United States. But had their feelings changed since then?

First, George and Laura had to figure out what they themselves wanted to do. Both of them felt that if George were to seek the presidency and be defeated, it would be easy enough for them to return to their normal lives. "If I choose to run and lose, so be it," George told a reporter. "I'll finish my term as governor and be a happy guy." He also said that becoming president was not something he had always wanted to do. "It wasn't on my radar screen," he says. Laura also admits that being the wife of the president was not what she had planned. She had adjusted nicely to the high-profile position of first lady of Texas, but she was not necessarily ready to be first lady of the United States. "It's sort of a stretch for me, because I could just as soon, you know, hang around and work in the yard," she told George.

Making their daughters comfortable with the decision was another matter. "You don't have to talk to the press," Laura assured them. "You don't have to do anything you don't want to do." George promised them that he would do whatever it took to ensure their privacy. "We'll just make it clear to everybody that my girls are off-limits to the press. Period," he said. Besides, they realized, they would be away at college; they wouldn't be living at the White House. Soon they were convinced that they would be able

George became the Republican Party's candidate for president at the Republican National Convention in August 2000. (Getty Images)

to lead relatively normal lives, even if their father were to become president.

In October 1999, a black-tie dinner was held at Southern Methodist University. At the event, Laura was honored with a Distinguished Alumni award. The affair was held the same night as an important campaign debate in New Hampshire. George chose to accompany Laura to the event at SMU rather than participate in the debate. When a reporter asked him why he had passed up the debate to attend the SMU event, he answered simply, "Because I love my wife."

The Road to the White House

Unsurprisingly, George won the Republican presidential nomination. As Laura suggested, he chose Dick Cheney as his running mate for vice president. Dick Cheney had been the secretary of defense during George Sr.'s administration.

Most of Laura's support for George had been behind the scenes until he won the nomination. But at the Republican National Convention in July 2000, she made her national political debut on prime-time television. Laura was very nervous about making the speech, and she opened the speech by admitting so. "I'm so thrilled. And I'm honored to be here. And I have to say I'm just a little bit overwhelmed to help open the convention that will nominate my husband for president of the United States." Then she quipped, "You know I'm completely objective when I say you've made a great choice."

The Republican National Convention was a very different setting from Laura's previous speaking venues, yet the topic of the speech was the same: education. Laura told the nation that her husband would make education one of his priorities. She backed this up with results of tests that had been performed in Texas schools. The tests indicated that the education reforms under George's administration had been successful. Now, Laura said, it was time for him to improve the education system throughout the country.

As it turned out, Laura had little reason to be nervous about making the speech. Lawrence O'Donnell Jr., a writer for *New York*, later said that Laura's speech was "the best ever by a first-lady-in-waiting."

George was now officially a presidential candidate. The next step for him was to turn his efforts toward his campaign against the Democratic nominee, Vice President Al Gore. Laura occasionally accompanied George on campaign stops around the country, but there was something that linked her to home even when she was traveling. It was the ranch they had recently bought in Crawford, a Texas town with a population of only 700. They had paid $1.3 million for the property, which spread for more than 1,500 acres. George and Laura knew they might need an occasional escape from the pressures of campaigning, and the ranch gave them that. Designing the ranch had become a project for Laura. So even when she was on a plane, thousands of miles from home, she flipped through design magazines, searching for ideas for their new home. Perhaps this helped her feel a bit closer to home.

The presidential campaign, however, would not be as enjoyable. Things got nasty as Republicans and Democrats engaged in mudslinging. The Democratic opponents were publicizing "dirt" on George, including his former problems with drinking. Laura had been worried about such campaign tactics from the start. She told a reporter about her concerns regarding campaigning. "I was worried about its impact on our family. I knew it would be hard to see someone I love criticized."

The family overcame that hurt to experience something even more stressful: a wait of more than a month before the official results of the election would be announced. On election day, Laura and George voted at the polls in Texas. At the end of the day, they gathered with their daughters and with George's parents to wait for the election results. George sat beside Laura in the living room of the Governor's Mansion, often with his arm around her. It had been a long and difficult election, and now all they could do was wait.

The initial results were not encouraging. Al Gore, George's Democratic opponent, was winning in many states. But the race was very close. Soon all eyes were on the state of Florida. It was clear that whichever candidate won in Florida would win the election. Tension mounted in the Governor's Mansion, but George Sr. noticed how Laura was able to keep his son calm. "Golly, she sure can calm him down," he says.

Finally, at 2:15 A.M. Eastern Standard Time, the TV networks declared Bush the winner of Florida—and therefore of the election. George hugged his wife while everyone else in the room jumped up and cheered. Then he turned to his father, and George Jr. and George Sr. wept in each other's arms.

Soon, Vice President Al Gore called George to concede to him—to acknowledge that George had won the vote. "You're a good man," George told him.

George Sr. later talked about how Laura was always able to keep her composure, even during that extremely stressful night. "It was a savage, horrible period. But she never got rattled, never got vindictive."

But at least in one case, it seemed that this was not entirely true. After Al Gore's first phone call to George, votes were still being counted. Over the next hour, the networks showed that George's lead was getting smaller and smaller. At 3:45 A.M., George received another call from his Democratic opponent. "Florida is too close to call," Al Gore said. "Let me make sure I understand. You're calling me to retract your concession?" George said angrily. "There's no reason to get snippy," Gore responded. Laura would normally be the first to calm George down. But this time, even she was angry. One of George's senior staff members later said about Laura, "It takes a lot to make her angry, but that phone call from Gore did it."

The results were not finalized that night. Some voters in Florida were charging that they had not been allowed to vote. Others said that the ballots were hard to understand.

In addition, the final tally of votes showed that George had won by a very small margin. By Florida law, the votes had to be recounted. So George and Laura and the rest of the Bush family had to wait even longer.

The next five weeks were enormously stressful. Many of the counties in Florida had to recount their votes. The country grew very divided as these recounts were started and stopped by the Florida courts. Supporters from both sides of the campaign began protesting. Finally, the case went to the United States Supreme Court. A majority of justices declared that the recounts should stop. The highest court in the country declared that George W. Bush, not Vice President Al Gore, would be the 43rd commander-in-chief of the United States.

Perhaps the presidential election of 2000 was an indication of what George W. Bush's presidency would be like. It was a roller coaster of high hopes and disappointments, a time of uncertainty, and a time of unexpected national and global challenges. But through it all, Laura continued to be a calming influence on George.

As Laura began her time as first lady of the United States, a journalist asked her whether she would be more like her mother-in-law, Barbara Bush, or her predecessor, Hillary Rodham Clinton. "I think I'll just be Laura Bush," she replied. Indeed, she continued to be Laura Bush, remaining an active advocate of important issues.

Being Laura Bush

One of those issues that have always been important to the former teacher and librarian is education. Laura worked hard to promote the No Child Left Behind (NCLB) Act as part of the president's education reforms. The NCLB Act is a $4 billion effort to recruit, prepare, and train teachers. It is considered one of the greatest federal investments ever. The NCLB Act requires schools to improve the quality of their education from year to year. To make sure this is happening, students take state tests more frequently. This helps the government track the success of different schools and see where more help is needed. Usually, disadvantaged students do much worse on state tests than children in better neighborhoods. ("Disadvantaged" students are students whose poverty, race, ethnicity, disabilities, or limited understanding of English make education more difficult for them.) An important goal of the NCLB Act is to help disadvantaged students get as good an education as students from schools in better neighborhoods get.

Through the NCLB Act, states must prove that the education their schools provide is improving and that they are meeting standards in reading and math. The government gets involved to help states that do not show improvement.

An important component of the NCLB Act is to use education programs that have been shown to be highly effective. The Reading First program, for example, gives reading teachers in early grades the tools they need to teach reading effectively. The U.S. Department of Education is developing a database of the best information on what works in teaching reading. The information will be available to teachers and schools on the Internet.

The NCLB Act funds several important programs. One of these is Ready to Read, Ready to Learn, a program of the First Lady's Family Literacy Initiative. Laura and her mother-in-law Barbara had begun the literacy initiative during Laura's first term as first lady of Texas. In July 2001—only six months after her husband had been sworn in as president—it was a topic of a meeting that Laura organized called the White House Summit on Early Childhood Cognitive Development. Many experts and important officials attended the meeting to discuss the best ways to help young children learn.

In a letter to the U.S. Department of Education, Laura points out the importance of reading for young children. "My experiences as a mother and an elementary school teacher have taught me that children that are ready to read are ready to learn," she writes. "As first lady, I will work tirelessly to make sure that every child gains the basic skills to be successful in school and in life."

There are two goals of Ready to Read, Ready to Learn. One goal is early childhood cognitive development. All children, according to the program, should be ready to read and learn when they enter their first classroom. The second goal is teacher preparation and recruitment. Achieving this goal means that trained, qualified teachers will be available in all schools, even in underprivileged neighborhoods.

There are several programs that help accomplish the goal of early childhood cognitive development. The Margaret Cone Center, for instance, is in a very poor neighborhood in Dallas. A reading professor at Southern Methodist University, the college from which Laura received her bachelor's degree, developed a program called Language Enrichment Activities Program (LEAP). Through this program, children at the Margaret Cone Center enjoy fun activities that improve their language and vocabulary skills. Another program that aids early childhood development is Reach Out and Read, a non-profit organization founded at Boston Medical Center. Reach Out and Read gets children's doctors involved with literacy. Through this program, pediatricians encourage parents to read to their children, and volunteers read aloud to children in waiting rooms.

Programs that work toward the second goal of Ready to Read, Ready to Learn include the New Teacher Project; Teach for America; Transition to Teaching; and the Troops to Teachers programs. These programs often recruit people who would not otherwise be teachers and place them in schools where they are needed the most, such as in inner cities and rural areas. For example, through the New Teacher Project, professionals in other careers become well-trained teachers. Teach for America recruits the best students from colleges and universities in the United States to become teachers. The Transition to Teaching program helps school districts find qualified teachers in their area. Even people in the military participate in Ready to Read, Ready to Learn programs: Troops to Teachers recruits retired and retiring servicemen and servicewomen to teach. Most teachers recruited through the Troops to Teachers program have extensive backgrounds in math, science, or engineering.

In addition to programs in the classroom, Ready to Read, Ready to Learn involves programs in the mail. *Healthy Start, Grow Smart* magazines are for parents of newborns. The magazines give parents important information about child health, safety, nutrition, and cognitive development. There is a different magazine for each stage of infancy, from newborn through 12 months of age. It is published in English and Spanish, and each month it is mailed to mothers of newborns who receive Medicaid services.

Ready to Read, Ready to Learn isn't the only federal program Laura promoted that, like her, had its roots in Texas.

First Lady of the United States • 73

In 1996, while she was first lady of Texas, Laura started the Texas Book Festival to honor authors from Texas. In its first four years, the festival earned $1 million for libraries in Texas. As first lady of the United States, Laura realized that a similar program could be successful on the national level, so she started the National Book Festival. The first festival, sponsored by Laura and the Library of Congress, was held on September 8, 2001. Approximately 30,000 people attended the event to hear readings by award-winning authors from across the country.

While the goal of the Texas Book Festival is to raise funds for libraries, the National Book Festival is not a fundraising event. Instead, its goal is to honor American authors and raise awareness about the importance of reading and literacy. "It's just a day for all of us to celebrate American authors and, of course, to celebrate reading," Laura explains.

In an interview on the day of the first National Book Festival, Laura related a story that reminded her of the importance of advocating issues as a first lady. Linda Gale, the wife of former Texas Governor Mark White, told her, "Laura, you just don't know what a forum you have when your husband is governor or president." Laura said in the interview, "And I know that. And I think that's why we've already had the very successful early childhood education summit last week and announced the National Book

Festival today. So I think I've actually taken very good advantage of the time I've had here."

The first National Book Festival featured readings and book signings by approximately 40 authors and book illustrators, including Stephen Ambrose, Scott Turow, and Sue Grafton. It also included storytelling, music, discussions, and demonstrations of new technologies. Storybook characters such as Wilbur and Charlotte from *Charlotte's Web*, Peter Rabbit, Puss in Boots, and Dr. Seuss's the Cat in the Hat strolled the grounds of the Library of Congress and the U.S. Capitol, where the festival was held. Children had their pictures taken with characters Clifford the Big Red Dog and Arthur. Professional basketball players, including Dikembe Mutombo and Nate "Tiny" Archibald, were also on hand. They helped promote the National Basketball Association's Read to Achieve Program, a year-round campaign to help young people develop a lifelong love for reading and to encourage adults to read regularly to children.

On October 12, 2002, the second National Book Festival was held. Seventy award-winning authors, illustrators, and storytellers participated in the event. Among them were Norman Bridwell, who created the *Clifford the Big Red Dog* series of books, and mystery author Mary Higgins Clark. Levar Burton, host of the PBS Kids series *Reading Rainbow*, hosted two presentations for children's literacy. The 2002 festival was attended by 45,000 people, including

Laura is the founder of the National Book Festival. Here she is pictured at the 2002 festival with Lyudmila Putina, wife of Vladimir Putin, president of the Russian Federation. (Associated Press)

Lyudmila Putina, wife of Vladimir Putin, president of the Russian Federation.

The third annual National Book Festival, held on October 4, 2003, featured more than 80 award-winning and nationally known authors, illustrators, poets, and storytellers. An equally wide variety of authors participated, including children's authors Stan and Jan Berenstain (*The*

Berenstain Bears series), R. L. Stine (the *Goosebumps* series for young adults), and adult mystery writer James Patterson. More than 60,000 attended the festival in 2003, which means that each year it has attracted approximately 50 percent more people than the year before.

The same year that Laura co-sponsored the first National Book Festival, she also helped create the Laura Bush Foundation for America's Libraries. The foundation raises funds to make a wider variety of books available in school libraries. In 2003, the Laura Bush Foundation awarded nearly $640,000 to schools so that they could purchase books for their libraries.

Laura also began hosting a White House literary series called "White House Salute to America's Authors." The series honors the lives and works of many respected American authors, including Mark Twain and the writers of the Harlem Renaissance. At each event of the series, scholars, students, and educators discuss the country's important writers. Getting all Americans, especially children, interested in reading great works is an important goal of this project. It is yet another way that Laura, as a former teacher and librarian, shares her love of reading with Americans.

7

A NEW CHALLENGE

Teacher and librarian are not the most important roles that Laura has ever held in her life and brought to her role as first lady. The terrorist attacks of September 11, 2001, in which more than 3,000 people lost their lives, brought her talents as a nurturing mother to the national spotlight.

That morning, Laura planned to speak to a Senate subcommittee about early childhood education. The head of the subcommittee was Senator Edward Kennedy, brother of John F. Kennedy, whose assassination in 1963 Laura remembers as "the most traumatic time in [her] childhood." By the time the White House limousine arrived at Capitol Hill, the second plane had hit the World Trade Center. The meeting was immediately postponed, and Laura and Senator Kennedy went to his office. "Words can't describe the depth of feeling I had, being with President Kennedy's brother as our nation's heart was broken with another tragedy," Laura remembers of that morning. Later, she would say of her drive from the White House to Capitol Hill, "We all knew 'normal' would never again be what we knew it to be on September 10."

Explaining her concern for her family, she said later, "Like every parent, I called my children immediately as soon as I could get them, to reassure them. And then I called my own mother, just for the comfort of her voice."

Promoting education was also the president's plan that morning. George was in a classroom of an elementary school in Sarasota, Florida, where he was promoting the Putting Reading First initiative. He had heard about the first plane crashing into the World Trade Center, but like many others, he assumed it was a horrible accident. When the second plane hit the World Trade Center, however, people throughout the world realized that the situation was serious.

Chief of Staff Andrew Card approached George, who was listening to the students reading a story aloud. "A second plane has just hit the World Trade Center," he whispered into the president's ear. "America is under attack."

Perhaps drawing on what he had learned from his wife, George made sure he appeared calm so as not to upset the students. Shortly afterward, he left the school and boarded his jet, Air Force One.

Meanwhile, Secret Service agents were busy taking the Bush twins—Barbara at Yale University and Jenna at the

University of Texas—to safe locations. Anyone close to the president, they knew, could be a target when the country is being attacked.

Once aboard Air Force One, George inquired about his family. He was assured that his wife and daughters were safe, and then he called Laura. Her calming influence on him was once again evident, which George would later say "was a very reassuring thing." Next on Laura's list to comfort were her daughters, whom George would later describe as "freaked out" by the events.

According to White House reports, George wanted to return to Washington, but his advisers had told him it was too risky. He wanted to meet the National Security Council, the group of the president's advisers who discuss the country's safety and foreign policy. He was also anxious to see his family again. Though it was a time when they probably needed each other most, it wasn't until 7:00 P.M. that night that George and Laura were reunited.

In the days following the tragedies of September 11, Laura was called both "Comforter-in-Chief" (by *Us Weekly* magazine) and "Counselor in Chief" (by the *Washington Post*). Both of these names play on the alternative title for the leader of the United States: commander-in-chief. She was also called "First Mother" by the *New York Post*, a reference to her own title of first lady. Laura's calming influence had extended beyond her family, beyond her friends, and beyond even a classroom of children. She had soothed an entire nation when Americans needed her most. She did so by talking on television about how parents can explain to their children what happened and why. ("They need their parents to give them lots of hugs," she said.) She also visited people who had been injured during the attacks and families of people whose lives had been lost. She wrote letters to American schoolchildren—one for elementary school children and one for older students. She sent the letters to state superintendents of schools so that the letters could be read to all students.

Perhaps aware of the influence that her own calm nature has on people around her, Laura told Americans, "Children take their emotional cues from their parents. They need a very calm and relaxed atmosphere at home."

After September 11, 2001, George and Laura Bush started a tradition with their daughters. They call Jenna and Barbara every day to tell them that they love them, and if the girls don't answer the phone, they leave them this message: "This is our call to tell you, number one, we love you, and number two, we love you."

An Advocate for Afghanistan

The tragic events of September 11, 2001, had a profound effect on Laura, not only as a mother but also as a first lady. In the months following that day, she made several public speeches related to the terrorist attacks on New York and Washington. The focus of many of those speeches was on issues facing women and children in Afghanistan.

Afghanistan was on the minds of many Americans. They knew that the oppressive Afghan government, called the Taliban, was protecting terrorists—including a group called al-Qaeda, which was responsible for the attacks on America. al-Qaeda's leader, Osama bin Laden, was believed to be hiding in Afghanistan, but the Taliban refused to help the United States find him. As a result, the president authorized the U.S. military to invade Afghanistan and hunt for members of al-Qaeda.

It was with this emotional backdrop that Laura made a very important speech in November 2001. By making this speech, she became the only first lady in history to record a full presidential radio address. In it, Laura told the country about some of the other victims of terrorists: women and children in Afghanistan. Women and children faced cruel treatment under the Taliban. "Afghan women know, through hard experience, what the rest of the world is discovering: The brutal oppression of women is a central goal of the terrorists," she said. To explain the importance of protecting women and children around the world rather than just in the United States, she said, "Civilized people throughout the world are speaking out in horror—not only because our hearts break for the women and children in Afghanistan, but also because in Afghanistan we see the world the terrorists would like to impose on the rest of us." Laura pointed out that about three out of four Afghan people are malnourished, and that one in four children in Afghanistan would not live past the age of five, because health care was not available. She also said that under the Taliban regime, women could not be educated, have jobs, or leave the house alone.

Laura welcomes women from Afghanistan to the White House; Laura played an important role in publicizing the unfair treatment of women under the Taliban. (Landov)

Since Laura made that address, there have been many changes in Afghanistan. After U.S. troops invaded Afghanistan, they toppled the Taliban. They then began to help the Afghan people rebuild a more democratic society. Efforts such as Laura's radio address have raised awareness of the cruel treatment of Afghan women and children under the old Taliban regime. In March 2004, just over two years later, George Bush acknowledged this. In a speech at the White House, he spoke of the importance of that historic radio address and the progress that has been made since then.

> . . . you know, one of the interesting moments in our family came when [Laura] gave a radio address. She used the president's time to give a radio address, to speak to the women of Afghanistan. And it made a big difference in people's lives. And it was from that moment forward that she, personally, has dedicated time to make sure that people who have been enslaved are free, particularly women. And I'm proud of Laura's leadership.

Laura gave specific examples of how life had changed for people in Afghanistan through efforts of the United States. "Afghan women who were once virtual prisoners in their homes, unable to go to school or to work, are helping rebuild their country," she said. By 2004, however, women were involved in drafting a constitution for their country, and they are now able to serve in the country's government. Women lead local councils in more than 2,000 Afghan villages. In addition, Afghan women were able to vote in Afghanistan's presidential election in 2004. She also announced that in late 2004, the United States would reopen an American school in Afghanistan's capital, Kabul. "I'm also working with our government and the private sector to develop a teacher training institute that will help prepare more women teachers for Afghan schools," she added.

While Laura acknowledges the importance of protecting women and children around the world, she realizes that protecting women and children on a smaller scale is also important. As first lady of Texas, she promoted Greater Texas Community Partners, an organization for abused and neglected children. Through this organization, volunteers run Rainbow Rooms. Rainbow Rooms are places that provide free diapers, baby formula, and clothing for abused children. She also promoted the Adopt-a-Caseworker program, another component of the Community Partners organization. Through this program, churches, schools, and businesses "adopt" child-abuse caseworkers, providing them with similar supplies as well as emotional support.

A Woman Helping Women

Laura is also very active in raising awareness of women's health issues. Through the Heart Truth campaign, she promotes awareness of heart disease. Although it is often thought of as a "men's disease," more women than men die of heart disease every year. In fact, it is the number one killer of women in the United States. In addition, many people don't know that women's symptoms are often different from the symptoms that men experience, so women often don't go to the doctor right away. For these reasons, the emphasis of the Heart Truth campaign is on women, although the information is useful for men as well. And the campaign helps more than just potential victims of heart disease: It also helps their doctors. At a speech during American Heart Month in 2004, Laura related the story of a woman who went to the doctor with symptoms that were not typical of a man's heart attack. The doctor checked her vital signs and told her she was fine. "She had heard a Heart Truth campaign event, and she heard that women didn't have the same symptoms always as men," Laura said. "So she rushed to the hospital and she was, in fact, having a heart attack."

During American Heart Month in February 2003, as part of the Heart Truth campaign, Laura helped start the Red Dress Project. The project helped make the red dress a symbol to remind people of the risk of heart disease for women. The following year, from March to May 2004, the Heart Truth Road Show traveled in cities throughout the country to bring free risk-factor screenings, a stunning display of red dresses, and important heart-health information to women.

Clearly, Laura does more for important issues than give speeches about them. She also participates in Race for the Cure, a fund-raiser for breast cancer. The event is a program of the Susan G. Komen Breast Cancer Foundation, an organization that Laura's close friend, Nancy Brinker, started in memory of her sister. Laura had campaigned to raise awareness of breast cancer even before her time as first lady of Texas, and she continues her support of the cause as first lady of the United States.

The 2004 Election

Laura faced yet another campaign in 2004: her husband's campaign for reelection to a second term as president of the United States. In an interview a few months before election day, when asked whether she expected the campaign to be "tough," Laura acknowledged that campaigning was still difficult for her. "Every one of them [is]. They always are," she said. "And we've sure come to know that."

Although Laura was aware that campaigning with her husband would be unpleasant in some ways, she played

A New Challenge • 87

As first lady, Laura Bush has established herself as a powerful advocate of many important issues. (Landov)

a vital role in George's reelection efforts. The sacrifice paid off. On an election day when a record number of Americans voted for their president, voters reelected George W. Bush. "America has spoken," he said in his acceptance speech. Then, acknowledging the importance of his wife's patience, support, and selflessness, he added, "Laura is the love of my life. I'm glad you love her, too."

TIME LINE

1946 Born on November 4 in Midland, Texas

1950 At kindergarten, memorizes the first and last names of all the children in her class

1954 Decides she wants to be a teacher when she grows up

1958 Reads *Doak Walker: Three-Time All-American* and decides she wants to go to Southern Methodist University in Dallas

1963 While driving with friends, runs a stop sign and hits a car, killing her close friend and ex-boyfriend, Mike Douglas

1964 Enters college at Southern Methodist University

1968 Graduates from Southern Methodist University with bachelor's degree in education; takes a trip across Europe; becomes clerk at a Dallas insurance company and then lands a job as third-grade teacher in Dallas

1969 Becomes second-grade teacher in Houston

1970 Begins master's program in library sciences at University of Texas in Austin

1973 Graduates from University of Texas in Austin with a master of library science degree

1974 Becomes children's librarian at a Houston public library

1975 Moves back to Austin to work as librarian in an elementary school

1977 Meets George W. Bush in August; George and Laura get engaged three weeks later; George and Laura get married three months later, on November 5; Laura moves into George's home in Midland, but they begin George's campaign for Congress

1978 George loses his bid to become a congressman

1981 George's father, George H. Bush, becomes vice president of the United States; George and Laura begin process of adopting a child until Laura learns she is pregnant with twins; on November 25, 1981, Laura gives birth to Jenna and Barbara Bush

1987	Laura and her family move to Washington, D.C., to help George Sr. campaign for president
1989	Laura and her family move to Dallas, Texas; George becomes managing general partner of Texas Rangers baseball team
1992	George Sr. loses presidency to Bill Clinton
1993	George runs for governor of Texas; Laura helps with the campaign; Laura's father is diagnosed with Alzheimer's disease
1994	George wins election for governor of Texas
1995	Laura and her family move into the Governor's Mansion in Austin, Texas; Laura's father dies
1996	Organizes a group that creates the First Lady's Family Literacy Initiative, which includes the Ready to Read, Ready to Learn program; starts the Texas Book Festival
1998	George is reelected governor of Texas; George sells Texas Rangers baseball team for more than $15 million
1999	Awarded a Distinguished Alumni award at Southern Methodist University

2000 George accepts the Republican Party nomination for president; Laura gives her first national speech at the Republican National Convention; after a disputed election, the Supreme Court issues a ruling that makes George the president

2001 Laura and her family move to the White House in Washington, D.C.; Laura organizes the White House Summit on Early Childhood Cognitive Development; hosts the first National Book Festival; terrorist attacks on September 11; Laura makes historic radio address about women and children in Afghanistan

2002 Hosts the second National Book Festival

2003 Hosts White House literacy series called "White House Salute to America's Authors"; helps start the Red Dress Project to promote awareness of heart disease among women; hosts the third National Book Festival

2004 Assists in George's reelection campaign, which he wins

HOW TO BECOME AN ELEMENTARY SCHOOL TEACHER

THE JOB

Depending on the schools at which they teach, *elementary school teachers* teach grades one through six or eight. In smaller schools, grades may be combined. There are still a few one-room, one-teacher elementary schools in remote rural areas. In most cases, however, teachers instruct approximately 20–30 children of the same grade. They teach a variety of subjects in the prescribed course of study, including language, science, mathematics, and social studies. In the classroom, teachers use various methods to educate their students, such as reading to them, assigning group projects, and showing films for discussion. Teachers also use educational games to help their pupils come up with creative ways to remember lessons.

In the first and second grades, elementary school teachers cover the basic skills: reading, writing, counting, and telling time. With older students, teachers instruct history, geography, math, English, and handwriting. To capture attention and teach new concepts, they use arts and crafts projects, workbooks, music, and other interactive activities. In the upper grades, teachers assign written and oral reports and involve students in projects and competitions such as spelling bees, science fairs, and math contests. Although they are usually required to follow a curriculum designed by state or local administrators, teachers study new learning methods to incorporate into the classroom, such as using computers to surf the Internet.

"I utilize many different, some unorthodox, teaching tools," says Andrea LoCastro, a sixth-grade teacher in Clayton, New Jersey. "I have a lunchtime chess club. Students give up their recess to listen to classical music and play, or learn to play, chess." She has also found that role-playing activities keep her students interested in the various subjects. "We are studying ancient Greece," she says, "and I currently have my students writing persuasive essays as part of either Odysseus' legal team or the Cyclops' legal team. I intend to culminate the activity with a mock trial, Athenian style."

To create unique exercises and activities such as those LoCastro uses, teachers need to devote a fair amount of time to preparation outside of the classroom. They prepare daily lesson plans and assignments, grade papers and tests, and keep a record of each student's progress. Other responsibilities include communicating with parents through written reports and scheduled meetings, keeping their classroom orderly, and decorating desks and bulletin boards to keep the learning environment visually stimulating.

Elementary school teachers may also teach music, art, and physical education, but these areas are often covered by specialized teachers. *Art teachers* are responsible for developing art projects, procuring supplies, and helping students develop drawing, painting, sculpture, mural design, ceramics, and other artistic abilities. Some art teachers also teach students about the history of art and lead field trips to local museums. *Music teachers* teach music appreciation and music history. They direct organized student groups such as choruses, bands, or orchestras, or they guide music classes by accompanying them in singing songs or playing instruments. Often, music teachers are responsible for organizing school pageants, musicals, and plays. *Physical education teachers* help students develop physical skills such as coordination, strength, and stamina and social skills such as self-confidence and good sportsmanship. Physical education teachers often serve as sports coaches and may be responsible for organizing field days and intramural activities.

When working with elementary-aged children, teachers need to instruct social skills along with general school subjects. They serve as disciplinarians, establishing and enforcing rules of conduct to help students learn right from wrong. To keep the classroom manageable, teachers maintain a system of rewards and punishments to encourage students to behave, stay interested, and participate. In cases of classroom disputes, teachers must also be mediators, teaching their pupils to resolve their arguments peacefully.

Recent developments in school curricula have led to new teaching arrangements and methods. In some schools, one or more teachers work with students within a small age range instead of with particular grades. Other schools are adopting bilingual education, where students are instructed throughout the day in two languages by either a *bilingual teacher* or two separate teachers.

Many teachers find it rewarding to witness students develop and hone new skills and adopt an appreciation for learning. In fact, many teachers inspire their own students to later join the teaching profession themselves. "Teaching is not just a career," says LoCastro. "It is a commitment—a commitment to the 20-plus children that walk into your classroom door each September eager for enlightenment and fun."

REQUIREMENTS
High School
Follow your school's college preparatory program and take advanced courses in English, mathematics, science, history, and government to prepare for an education degree. Art, music, physical education, and extracurricular activities will contribute to a broad base of knowledge necessary to teach a variety of subjects. Composition, journalism, and communications classes are also important for developing your writing and speaking skills.

Postsecondary Training
All 50 states and the District of Columbia require public elementary education teachers to have a bachelor's degree in either education or the subject they plan to teach. Prospective teachers must also complete an approved training program. In the United States, there are more than 500 accredited teacher education programs, which combine subject and educational classes with work experience in the classroom.

Though programs vary by state, courses cover how to instruct language arts, mathematics, physical science, social science, art, and music. In addition, prospective teachers must take educational training courses such as philosophy of education, child psychology, and learning methods. To gain experience in the classroom, student teachers are placed in a school to work with a full-time teacher. During this training period, student teachers observe the ways in which lessons are presented and the classroom is managed, learn how to keep records of attendance and grades, and gain experience in handling the class, both under supervision and alone.

Some states require prospective teachers to have master's degrees in education and specialized technology training to keep them familiar with more modern teaching methods using computers and the Internet.

Certification or Licensing

Public school teachers must be licensed under regulations established by the state in which they are teaching. If a teacher moves to a new state, he or she has to comply with any other regulations in the new state to be able to teach, though many states have reciprocity agreements that make it easier for teachers to change locations.

Licensure examinations test prospective teachers for competency in basic subjects such as mathematics, reading, writing, teaching, and other subject-matter proficiency. In addition, many states are moving toward a performance-based evaluation for licensing. In this case, after passing the teaching examination, prospective teachers are given provisional licenses. Only after proving themselves capable in the classroom are they eligible for a full license.

Another growing trend spurred by recent teacher shortages is alternative licensure arrangements. For those who have a bachelor's degree but lack formal education courses and training in the classroom, states can issue a provisional license. These workers immediately begin teaching under the supervision of a licensed educator for one to two years and take education classes outside of their working hours. Once they have completed the required coursework and gained experience in the classroom, they are granted a full license. This flexible licensing arrangement has helped to bring additional teachers into school systems needing instructors.

Other Requirements

Many consider the desire to teach to be a calling. This calling is based on a love of children and a dedication to their welfare. If you want to become a teacher, you must respect children as individuals who possess personalities, strengths, and weaknesses of their own. You must also be patient and self-disciplined to manage a large group independently. Teachers make a powerful impression on children, so they need to serve as good role models. "Treat students with kindness and understanding, rules and consequences," LoCastro suggests. "Be nice, yet strict. They'll love you for it."

EXPLORING

To explore a teaching career, look for leadership opportunities that involve working with children. You might find summer work as a counselor in a summer camp, as a leader of a scout troop, or as an assistant in a public park or community center. Look for opportunities to tutor younger students or coach children's athletic teams. Local community theaters may need directors and assistants for summer children's productions. Day care centers often hire high school students for late afternoon and weekend work.

EMPLOYERS

There are more than 1.5 million elementary school teachers employed in the United States. Teachers are needed at public and private institutions, including parochial schools and Montessori schools, which focus more on the child's own initiatives. Teachers are also needed in day care centers that offer full-day elementary programs and charter schools, which are smaller, deregulated institutions that receive public funding. Although rural areas maintain schools, more teaching positions are available in urban or suburban areas.

STARTING OUT

After obtaining a college degree, finishing the student-teaching program, and becoming certified, prospective teachers have many avenues for finding a job. College placement offices and state departments of education maintain listings of job openings. Many local schools advertise teaching positions in newspapers. Another option is directly contacting the administration in the schools in which you'd like to work. While looking for a full-time position, you can work as a substitute teacher. In urban areas that have many schools, you may be able to find full-time substitute work.

ADVANCEMENT

As teachers acquire experience or additional education, they can expect higher wages and more responsibilities. Teachers with leadership skills and an interest in administrative work may advance to serve as principals or supervisors, though the number of these positions is limited and competition is fierce. Others may advance to work as *senior* or *mentor teachers* who assist less experienced staff.

Another move may be into higher education, teaching education classes at a college or university. For most of these positions, additional education is required.

Other common career transitions are into related fields. With additional preparation, teachers can become librarians, editors, reading specialists, or counselors.

"I intend to continue teaching as my career," says Andrea LoCastro. "I am not at all interested in moving up to administration. I will, however, pursue a master's in teaching after receiving tenure."

EARNINGS

According to the Bureau of Labor Statistics, the average annual salary for elementary school teachers was $44,080 in 2002. The lowest 10 percent earned $24,960 or less; the highest 10 percent earned $68,530 or more.

The American Federation of Teachers reports that the average salary for beginning teachers with a bachelor's degree was $30,719 in the 2001–02 school year. The estimated average salary of all public elementary and secondary school teachers was $44,367.

Teachers often supplement their earnings through teaching summer classes, coaching sports, sponsoring clubs, or other extracurricular work. More than half of all teachers belong to unions such as the American Federation of Teachers or the National Education Association. These unions bargain with schools over contract conditions such as wages, hours, and benefits. Depending on the state, teachers usually receive a retirement plan, sick leave, and health and life insurance. Some systems grant teachers sabbatical leave.

WORK ENVIRONMENT

Most teachers are contracted to work 10 months out of the year, with a two-month vacation during the summer. During their summer break, many continue their education to renew or upgrade their teaching licenses and earn higher salaries. Teachers in schools that operate year-round work eight-week sessions with one-week breaks in between and a five-week vacation in the winter.

Teachers work in generally pleasant conditions, although some older schools may have poor heating or electrical systems. The work can seem confining, requiring them to remain in the classroom throughout most of the day. Although the job is not overly strenuous, dealing with busy children all day can be tiring and trying. Teachers must stand for many hours each day, do a lot of talking, and show energy and enthusiasm, and they may have to handle discipline problems. But, according to Andrea LoCastro, problems with students are usually overshadowed by their successes. "Just knowing a child is learning something because of you is the most rewarding feeling, especially when you and the child have struggled together to understand it."

OUTLOOK

According to the *Occupational Outlook Handbook*, employment opportunities for teachers (grades K–12) are expected to grow as fast as the average for all occupations through 2012. The need to replace retiring teachers will provide many opportunities nationwide.

The demand for teachers varies widely depending on geographic area. Inner-city schools characterized by poor working conditions and low salaries often suffer a shortage of teachers. In addition, more opportunities exist for those who specialize in a subject in which it is harder to attract qualified teachers, such as mathematics, science, or foreign languages.

The National Education Association believes it will be a difficult challenge to hire enough new teachers to meet rising enrollments and replace the large number of retiring teachers, primarily because of low teacher salaries. Higher salaries along with other necessary changes, such as smaller classroom sizes and safer schools, will be necessary to attract new teachers and retain experienced ones. Other challenges for the profession involve attracting more men into teaching. The percentage of male teachers continues to decline.

In order to improve education, drastic changes are being considered by some districts. Some private companies are managing public schools in the hope of providing better facilities, faculty, and equipment. Teacher organizations are concerned about taking school management away from communities and turning it over to remote corporate headquarters.

Charter schools and voucher programs are two other controversial alternatives to traditional public education. Publicly funded charter schools are not guided by the rules and regulations of traditional public schools. Some view these schools as places of innovation and improved educational methods; others see them as ill-equipped and unfairly funded with money that could better benefit local school districts. Vouchers, which exist only in a few cities, use public tax dollars to allow students to attend private schools. In theory, the vouchers allow for more choices in education for poor and minority students. Teacher organizations see some danger in giving public funds to unregulated private schools.

TO LEARN MORE ABOUT ELEMENTARY SCHOOL TEACHERS

BOOKS

Levine, Mel. *A Mind at a Time*. New York: Simon and Schuster, 2003.

Sawyer, Emmet, et al. *Teacher Career Starter*. 2d ed. New York: Learning Express, 2002.

Shalaway, Linda. *Learning to Teach . . . Not Just for Beginners*. New York: Scholastic, 1999.

Williamson, Bonnie. *A First-Year Teacher's Guidebook*. 2d ed. Dynamic Teaching Company, 1998.

Wong, Harry K., and Rosemary Tripi Wong. *The First Days of School: How to Be an Effective Teacher*. Harry K. Wong Publishers, 2001.

ORGANIZATIONS AND WEBSITES

For information about careers, education, and union membership, contact the following organizations:

American Federation of Teachers
555 New Jersey Avenue, NW
Washington, DC 20001
Tel: 202-879-4400
Email: online@aft.org
http://www.aft.org

National Council for Accreditation of Teacher Education
2010 Massachusetts Avenue, NW, Suite 500
Washington, DC 20036-1023
Tel: 202-466-7496
Email: ncate@ncate.org
http://www.ncate.org

National Education Association
1201 16th Street, NW
Washington, DC 20036
Tel: 202-833-4000
http://www.nea.org

HOW TO BECOME A LIBRARIAN

THE JOB

Librarians perform a number of tasks depending on their specialties. Some librarians may focus entirely on user services, while others are concerned with technical or administrative services. Depending on the needs of their departments or institutions, librarians may perform a combination of these tasks, or take care of even more specific duties within their specialty. Some specific types of librarians in each category are noted in the following paragraphs, but this is not an exhaustive list. If one of these areas interests you, be sure to contact a library school for information about additional opportunities.

The librarian working in user services helps patrons find materials and use resources effectively. This type of librarian should be thoroughly acquainted with all materials in the library, from card and online catalogs to reference books. *Reference librarians* advise users and help them find information they are seeking in encyclopedias, almanacs, reference books, computerized information databases, or other sources. They also have access to special materials that may be filed in areas not open to the public or kept off-site.

Often, librarians in user services may choose to work with a special age group. *Children's librarians* help children select books, teach them about the library, and conduct story hours. *Young-adult librarians* perform similar services for junior and senior high school students. Instead of story hours, however, they plan programs of interest to young adults, such as creative writing workshops, film discussion groups, music concerts, and photography classes. *Adult services* librarians work with the adult population. They may help conduct education programs in community development, creative arts, public affairs, problems of the aging, and home and family.

Law librarians are professionally trained librarians who work in legal settings such as private law firms, government libraries, and law schools.

Medical librarians, also known as *information specialists*, help manage health information. They are employed in libraries or information centers in hospitals and other medical facilities, public libraries, government agencies, research centers, colleges and universities, and pharmaceutical, publishing, biotechnology, and insurance companies.

Music librarians perform many of the same duties as traditional librarians but specialize in managing materials related to music. They are employed at large research libraries; colleges, universities, and conservatories; public libraries; radio and television stations; and musical societies and foundations. They also work for professional bands or orchestras and music publishing companies.

Library media specialists work with young people in school settings. They select materials useful to students in their class work, teach them to use the library media center effectively, help them with assignments, and work with teachers on research. Also known as *audiovisual librarians*, library media specialists (who must also be certified as teachers) select and maintain films, videotapes, slides, prints, records, cassettes, DVDs, compact discs, and other nonprint materials and supervise the purchase and maintenance of the equipment needed to use these materials.

Community outreach librarians or *bookmobile librarians* bring library services to outlying areas or to special communities such as nursing homes or inner-city housing projects. These librarians bring resources to communities that do not have easy access to library services.

The technical tasks of the librarian may include ordering, cataloging, and classifying materials according to the Dewey Decimal, Library of Congress, or other system, and librarians involved with these technical services might not deal with the public at all. These librarians select and order all books, periodicals, audiovisual materials, and other items for the library; this entails evaluating newly published materials as well as seeking out older ones. Many libraries have added records, audio- and videotapes, compact discs, DVDs, films, filmstrips, slides, maps, art pieces, and photographs to their loan services. The selection and purchase of these is also the responsibility of the librarian. The librarian, therefore, considerably influences the quality and extent of a library collection.

All new additions to the library must be cataloged by title, author, and subject in either card or computerized catalog files. Labels and card pockets must be placed on the items, and they must then be properly shelved. Books and other materials must be kept in good condition and, when necessary, repaired or replaced. Librarians are also charged with purchasing, maintaining, and evaluating the circulation system. Considerable technical knowledge of computer systems may be necessary in deciding upon the extent and scope of the proper circulation for the library. The process of circulating books, such as stamping due dates, collecting fines, and tracking down overdue materials, however, is usually handled by nonprofessional library staff such as work-study students, part-time employees, and library technicians.

Acquisitions librarians choose and buy books and other media for the library. They must read product catalogs and reviews of new materials as part of the acquisitions decision process. They do not work with the public but do deal with publishers and wholesalers of new books, booksellers of out-of-print books, and distributors of audiovisual materials. When the ordered materials arrive, *catalog librarians*, with the aid of *classifiers*, classify the items by subject matter, assign classification numbers, and prepare cards or computer records to help users locate the materials. Since many libraries have computerized the acquisitions and cataloging functions, it is now possible for the user to retrieve materials faster. Many automated libraries are phasing out bulky card catalogs and providing users with small computer terminals instead.

Bibliographers usually work in research libraries, compiling lists of books, periodicals, articles, and audiovisual materials on selected topics. They also recommend the purchase of new materials in their special fields. *Information scientists*, or *technical librarians*, are specialists trained in computer sciences. More and more libraries today are tied into remote computer databases through their computer terminals, making it unnecessary for a library to house all the materials users may request. Information scientists design systems for storing and retrieving information. They also develop procedures for collecting, organizing, interpreting, and classifying information.

Circulation librarians, with the help of clerical workers and stack attendants, manage the records of books and materials that are borrowed and returned and make sure that the materials are returned to the appropriate place in the library. *Conservation librarians* are charged with protecting and lengthening the life of the library collection. These librarians plan for the future, preparing for circumstances that might threaten the collections.

Administrative services librarians watch over the management of all areas of the library. They supervise library personnel and prepare budgets. They are also responsible for public relations and represent the library within its community as well as in such policy-making organizations as state or national library associations. Ultimately, administrators make sure that the library is constantly cultivating and expanding its resources to best serve the needs of its community.

The *library director* is at the head of a typical library organizational scheme. This individual sets library policies and plans and administers programs of library services, usually under the guidance of a governing body, such as a board of directors or board of trustees. Library directors have overall responsibility for the operation of a library system. Among their many duties, they coordinate the activities of the *chief librarians*, who supervise branch libraries or individual departments, such as the circulation, general reference, or music departments; periodical reading room, or readers' advisory service. In a large public library, a chief librarian supervises a staff of assistant librarians and division heads while administering and coordinating the functions of the library.

The *assistant librarians* often consult with (and report to) the chief librarian or library director regarding policy decisions for their area. They also train, schedule, and supervise *library technicians*, sometimes called *library assistants*. Library technicians work in all areas of library services. They assist patrons in the library or on the telephone, and they provide information on library services, facilities, and rules. They also catalog materials, prepare orders of materials and books, maintain files, work on checkouts, and perform many other varieties of jobs within specialized areas such as audiovisual or data processing.

REQUIREMENTS

High School

If you are interested in becoming a librarian, be sure to take a full college preparatory course load. Focus on classes in history, English, speech, and foreign languages if you are going into user services. If you plan on working in a special library, take classes related to that specialty. For instance, if science is your interest, take courses such as anatomy, biology, chemistry, and physics. Learning how to use a computer and conduct basic research in a library is essential. Developing these skills will not only aid in your future library work but also help you in college and in any other career options you might pursue.

Postsecondary Training

Consider enrolling in a liberal arts college to get a broad educational background, since librarians should be familiar with numerous subject areas. While an undergraduate, you can begin considering what area of librarianship you wish to pursue, and focus on those courses. Many library schools don't require specific undergraduate courses for acceptance, but a good academic record and reading knowledge of at least one foreign language is usually required. You should also consider taking classes that strengthen your skills in communications, writing, research methods, collection organization, and customer service, as well as maintenance and conservation. More than half of the accredited library schools do not require any introductory courses in library science at the undergraduate level. It would be wise, though, to check with schools for specific requirements.

Upon receiving your bachelor's degree, you will need to earn a master's degree to become a librarian. The degree is generally known as the master of library science (MLS), but in some institutions it may be referred to by a different title, such as the master of library and information science (MLIS). You should plan to attend a graduate school of library and information science that is accredited by the American Library Association (ALA). Currently, there are 56 ALA-accredited programs. Some libraries do not consider job applicants who attended a nonaccredited school.

During the year of graduate study, you will take courses in reference work, cataloging, classification, computers, library organizations, and administration. Other courses focus on the history of books and printing and on issues of censorship and intellectual freedom. Information scientists focus on courses in computer sciences, mathematics, and systems analysis. Many library schools have work-study programs where students take classes while gaining practical experience in a library.

Specialized librarians, such as law, pharmaceutical, or geology librarians, must have a very strong background in the subject in which they wish to work. Most have a degree in their subject specialization in addition to their MLS. In some cases, a graduate or professional degree in the subject is especially attractive to prospective employers. For work in research libraries, university libraries, or special collections, a doctorate may be required. A doctorate is commonly required for the top administrative posts of these types of libraries, as well as for faculty positions in graduate schools of library science.

Certification or Licensing

In many states, school librarians, also referred to as library media specialists, are required to earn teacher's certification in addition to preparation as a librarian. They may also be required to earn a master's degree in education. Various state, county, and local governments have set up other requirements for education and certification. You should contact the school board in the area in which you are interested in working for specific requirements. Your public library system should also have that information readily available.

The ALA is currently developing a voluntary certification program to recognize individuals who have demonstrated knowledge and skills in library science and to promote professional development.

Other Requirements

Librarians are often expected to take part in community affairs, cooperating in the preparation of exhibits, presenting book reviews, and explaining library use to community organizations. You will need to be a leader in developing the cultural tastes of the library patrons. Librarians who deal with the public should have strong interpersonal skills, tact, and patience. An imaginative, highly motivated, and resourceful personality is very valuable. A zeal for problem solving is another desirable quality. Library specialists, too, must have particular personal qualifications; for example, young-adult librarians must have a real liking for teenagers, and bookmobile librarians should feel comfortable traveling to outlying areas and dealing with all sorts of people.

Librarians involved with technical services should be detail-oriented, have good planning skills, and be able to think analytically. All librarians should have a love for information and be willing to master the techniques for obtaining and presenting knowledge. They must also be prepared to master constantly changing technology.

EXPLORING

There are several ways you can explore the field of librarianship. First of all, high school students have their own personal experiences with the library: reading, doing research for class projects, or just browsing. If this experience sparks an interest in library work, you can talk with a school or community librarian whose own experiences in the field can provide a good idea of what goes on behind the scenes. Some schools may have library clubs you can join to learn about library work. If one doesn't exist, you could consider starting your own library club.

Once you know you are interested in library work, you might be able to work as an assistant in the school library media center or find part-time work in a local public library. Such volunteer or paid positions may provide you with experience checking materials in and out at the circulation desk, shelving returned books, or typing title, subject, and author information on cards or in computer records. In college, you might be able to work as a technical or clerical assistant in one of your school's academic libraries.

Contact the American Library Association or another professional organization to inquire about student memberships. Most groups offer excellent mentoring opportunities as well. Finally, if you have an email account, sign up for one or more of the electronic mailing lists offered by these groups. These email lists are lists of professionals throughout the world who consult each other on special topics. ALA members monitor a number of listservs for members and nonmembers. By subscribing to one of these lists, you can discover what matters concern professional librarians today. Before you post your own comment or query, however, be sure you know the rules and regulations created by the list's moderator, and always be respectful of others.

EMPLOYERS

All types of libraries need library professionals. Public libraries, school libraries, library media centers, college or university libraries, research libraries, and other special libraries all employ librarians. Private industry and government departments have libraries that need staffing. Librarians also work outside of the traditional library setting.

A librarian can work for a small branch office of a major library or in a large library that services many counties. A librarian in a smaller library may have duties in all areas of librarianship: ordering, cataloging, shelving, and circulating materials, as well as acting as reference librarian. On the other hand, a librarian at a larger institution has a more specialized venue, such as a history section or map room.

Many universities have multiple libraries that serve different groups of people. The University of Chicago library system, for example, has a separate law library, a general reading collection library, a humanities and social sciences repository, a social services administration division, and four science libraries. Librarians at such an institution might work in administration overseeing the branches of the entire system or may deal with operations in one of the satellite areas.

Businesses and organizations also employ library professionals. Special librarians manage libraries for businesses, nonprofit corporations, and government agencies.

The materials collected usually pertain to subjects of particular interest to the organization. *Institution librarians* plan and direct library programs for residents and staff of institutions such as prisons, hospitals, and other extended-care facilities.

As the field of library and information services grows, librarians can find more work outside of the traditional library setting. Experienced information scientists may advise libraries or other agencies on information systems, library renovation projects, or other information-based issues. In addition, librarians act as *trainers* and *service representatives* for online database vendors, helping users use the information from online services.

STARTING OUT

In some cases, part-time work experience while in graduate school may turn into a full-time position upon graduation. Some employers, too, may allow an especially promising applicant to begin learning on the job before the library degree is conferred. Employers seeking new graduates often recruit through library schools. Most professional library and information science organizations have job listings that candidates can consult. Also, many online job search engines can help librarians find an appropriate position. Newspaper classifieds may be of some help in locating a job, although other approaches may be more appropriate to the profession.

Many librarians entering the workforce today are combining their experience in another career with graduate library and information science education. For example, a music teacher who plays trumpet in a band could mix her part-time teaching experience and her hobby with a degree in library science to begin a full-time career as a music librarian. Almost any background can be used to advantage when entering the field of librarianship.

Since school library media specialists work in elementary schools and high schools, they must apply directly to school boards. Individuals interested in working in library positions for the federal government can contact the human resources department or consult the website of the government agency where they are interested in working; for these government positions, applicants must take a civil service examination. Public libraries, too, are often under a civil service system of appointment.

ADVANCEMENT

The beginning librarian may gain experience by taking a job as an assistant. He or she can learn a lot from practical experience before attempting to manage a department or entire library. A librarian may advance to positions with greater levels of responsibility within the same library system, or a librarian may gain initial experience in a small library and then advance by transferring to a larger or more specialized library. Within a large library, promotions to higher positions are possible, for example, to the supervision of a department. Experienced librarians with the necessary qualifications may advance to positions in library administration. A doctorate is desirable for reaching top administrative levels, as well as for taking a graduate library school faculty position.

Experienced librarians, in particular those with strong administrative, computer, or planning backgrounds, may move into the area of information consulting. They use their expertise to advise libraries and other organizations on issues regarding information services. Other experienced librarians, especially those with computer experience, may also go into specialized areas of library work, becoming increasingly valuable to business and industry, as well as other fields.

EARNINGS

Salaries depend on such factors as the location, size, and type of library, the amount of experience the librarian has, and the responsibilities of the position. According to the U.S. Department of Labor, median annual earnings of librarians in 2002 were $43,090. Salaries ranged from less than $24,510 to more than $66,590. Librarians working in elementary and secondary school earned $45,660 in 2002, and those in colleges and universities earned about $45,600. Librarians employed in local government earned $37,970 in 2002.

WORK ENVIRONMENT

Most libraries are pleasant and comfortable places in which to assist those doing research, studying, or reading for pleasure. Librarians must do a considerable amount of reading to keep informed in order to serve library patrons. They must also strive to stay abreast of constantly changing technology, which may seem overwhelming at times.

Some librarians, such as reference or special librarians, may find the work demanding and stressful when they deal with users who are working under deadline pressure. Librarians working in technical services may suffer eyestrain and headaches from working long hours in front of a computer screen. On the average, librarians work between 35 and 40 hours per week.

There is, of course, some routine in library work, but the trend is to place clerical duties in the hands of library technicians and library assistants, freeing the professional librarian for administrative, research, personnel, and community services.

OUTLOOK

Overall, job opportunities for librarians will grow about as fast as the average for all jobs through 2012, according to the U.S. Department of Labor. The American Library Association predicts a serious shortage of librarians in the next five to 12 years, as one in four librarians is expected to retire in the next five to seven years, and approximately half will retire within 12 years.

Employment opportunities will be best in nontraditional library settings, such as information brokers, private corporations, and consulting firms. The outlook is good for those skilled in developing computerized library systems as well as for those with a strong command of foreign languages.

The expanding use of computers to store and retrieve information and to handle routine operations will require that librarians have strong computer skills, and in some cases these tasks, once performed solely by librarians, can now be performed by other library staff members. The automation of libraries will in no way replace librarians, however; personal judgment and knowledge will still be needed in libraries.

Many librarians will find employment as trainers, customer representatives, and sales representatives for information database vendors. The expansion of the Internet will create new occupational opportunities for librarians—opportunities with such titles as *Internet trainer, Internet consultant,* and *Internet coordinator.*

TO LEARN MORE ABOUT LIBRARIANS

BOOKS

Bannister, Barbara Farley. *Elementary School Librarian's Survival Guide.* Eugene, Oreg.: Center for Applied Research in Education, 1993.

Johnson, Doug. *The Indispensable Librarian: Surviving (and Thriving) in School Media Centers in the Information Age.* Worthington, Ohio: Linworth Publishing, 1997.

Mann, Thomas. *Library Research Models. A Guide to Classification, Cataloging, and Computers.* New York: Oxford University Press, 1994.

Mann, Thomas. *The Oxford Guide to Library Research.* New York: Oxford University Press, 1998.

ORGANIZATIONS AND WEBSITES

For career information, a list of accredited schools, information on scholarships and grants, and college student membership, contact

American Library Association
50 East Huron Street
Chicago, IL 60611
Tel: 800-545-2433
Email: membership@ala.org
http://www.ala.org

For information on information science careers, contact

American Society for Information Science and Technology
1320 Fenwick Lane, Suite 510
Silver Spring, MD 20910
Tel: 301-495-0900
Email: asis@asis.org
http://www.asis.org

For information on working in a specialized library, contact

Special Libraries Association
1700 18th Street, NW
Washington, DC 20009-2514
Tel: 202-234-4700
Email: sla@sla.org
http://www.sla.org

To receive information on librarianship in Canada, write
Canadian Library Association
328 Frank Street
Ottawa, ON K2P 0X8 Canada
Tel: 613-232-9625
Email: info@cla.ca
http://www.cla.ca

TO LEARN MORE ABOUT LAURA BUSH

BOOKS

Andersen, Christopher. *George and Laura: Portrait of an American Marriage.* New York: Avon Books, 2002.

Felix, Antonia. *Laura: America's First Lady, First Mother.* Avon, Mass.: Adams Media Corporation, 2003.

ARTICLES

"City of Midland," Midland.tx.us, Available online. URL: http://www.ci.midland.tx.us/index.html. Posted 2001.

"First Lady Laura Bush," whitehouse.gov. Available online. URL: http://www.whitehouse.gov/firstlady/.

"Interview with Laura Bush," *Living It Up with Ali & Jack*, February 6, 2004.

"Laura W. Bush," laurabushfoundation.org. Available online. URL: http://www.laurabushfoundation.org/mrsbush.html.

"Laura Bush Delivers Remarks at Republican National Convention," CNN.com. Available online. URL: http://www.cnn.com/ELECTION/2000/conventions/republican/transcripts/u010731.html. Posted July 31, 2000.

"The Laura Bush Foundation for America's Libraries," laurabushfoundation.org. Available online. URL: http://www.laurabushfoundation.org/foundation.html.

"National Teacher of the Year Award—Introduction of the President," whitehouse.gov. Available online. URL: http://www.whitehouse.gov/news/releases/2003/04/20030430-24.html. Posted April 30, 2001.

"SMU's Relationships with President George W. Bush, Laura Bush, and Vice President Dick Cheney," smu.edu. Available online. URL: http://www.smu.edu/newsinfo/releases/00171.html. Posted January 20, 2001.

"The Teaching of Laura Bush," readersdigest.com. Available online. URL: http://www.rd.com/common/nav/index.jhtml?articleId=9524826&channelId=5&subChannelId=19. Posted 2001.

Bruni, Frank. "For Laura Bush, a Direction She Never Wished to Go In." *New York Times*, July 31, 2000.

Levine, Ellen. "Laura Bush: An Intimate Conversation." *Good Housekeeping*. Available online. URL: http://magazines.ivillage.com/goodhousekeeping/myhome/friends/articles/0,,287164_561058,00.html. Posted February 2003.

Romano, Lois. "Laura Bush: A Twist on Traditional: Reluctant Celebrity Took Unconventional Route," *Washington Post*, May 14, 2000.

ORGANIZATIONS AND WEBSITES

Laura Bush Foundation
http://www.laurabushfoundation.org

Southern Methodist University
http://www.smu.edu

White House
http://www.whitehouse.gov

INDEX

Page numbers in *italics* indicate illustrations.

A

Adopt-a-Caseworker program 84
Afghanistan, women and children in 80–84, 91
ALA. *See* American Library Association (ALA)
al-Qaeda 81
Ambrose, Stephen 74
American Federation of Teachers 101–102, 106
American Library Association (ALA) 115, 116, 118, 124, 127
Archibald, Nate "Tiny" 74
Army Air Force Bombardier Training School 6

B

Barrett, Mrs. 10
Berenstain, Jan 75
Berenstain, Stan 75
bin Laden, Osama 81
Bohren, Gwyne Smith 12
Bridwell, Norman 74
Brinker, Nancy 86
Burton, Levar 74
Bush, Barbara (daughter) 41, 48, 59–60, 61–63, 78–79, 80, 89
Bush, Barbara (mother-in-law) *34, 35,* 36, 54, *55,* 68, 70
Bush, George H. W. (father-in-law)
    campaigns of 44, 46, 48, 59, 90
    Cheney and 64
    on daughter-in-law's composure 66, 67
    on Nixon 7
    personality of 57

133

Bush, George H. W.
(father-in-law) *(continued)*
  as president 44–45, 47
  on son's run for presidency 60
  at son's wedding *34*
  as vice president 38, 44, 89
Bush, George W. (husband)
  on art 56
  campaigns of 30, 34–37, *36,* 38–39, 47–49, 50, 61–68, 86–87, 89, 91
  children of 39–43, *42,* 61–63, 66, 79, 80, 89
  courtship and marriage 1, 7, 29–34, *34,* 38–40, 57–59, 89
  drinking problem of 43–44, 66
  on education 64–65, 69, 78
  on father-in-law 57
  on father's presidential campaigns 44–45, 46
  as governor 3, 22, *23,* 50–53, 59–60, 90
  memory of 9
  oil business of 37–38, 39, 43
  as president 68, 78–79, 80, 83, 86–87, 91
  at Republican National Convention (2000) *63*
  Texas Rangers owned by 45–46, 90
  on wife 1–2, 49, 58, 83, 87
  wife's influence on 48–49, 58–59, 66–67, 68, 78, 79
Bush, Jeb 60
Bush, Jenna (daughter) 41, 48, 59–60, 61–63, 78–79, 80, 89
Bush, Laura Welch *87*
  on Afghan women and children 3, 80–84, *82,* 91
  as art patron 56–57
  automobile accident of 16–18, 88
  birth 5, 88
  books and articles about 129–131
  calming influence of 49, 57–59, 66, 68, 77–78, 79–80
  on campaigns 18, 34–37, *36,* 46, 47–50, 61–68, 86–87, 89, 90, 91
  childhood 5–13, 88
  children of 39–43, *42,* 61–63, 66, 78–79, 80, 89
  at college 19–22, 25–26, 88, 89
  courtship and marriage 29–*34,* 34, 89
  on education 1, 2, 19–20, 49, 64–65, 69
  as first lady of Texas 3, 22, 47, 50–57, *52,* 59–60, 84, 90
  as first lady of United States 3, 68–87, 91
  foundation of 76, 131

in Junior League 39
as librarian 9, 26–28,
  29–30, 89
as literacy advocate 2, 27,
  39, 43, 53–56, 55, 69–76
memory of 8–9
on National Book Festival
  73–76, 75, 91
on politics 1, 7, 58
post-college European trip
  of 22–23
on public speaking 1–2, 4,
  37, 49, 53–54, 64–65
at Republican National
  Convention (2000) 1, 2,
  11, 63, 64–65
SMU Distinguished Alumni
  Award to 22, 23, 63–64, 90
as teacher 24–25, 89
on teachers 2–3, 24, 69–72,
  84
as teenager 13, 14–19
after terrorist attacks of
  9/11 77–78, 79–81
time line of 88–91
on "White House Salute to
  America's Authors" 76, 91
on White House Summit on
  Early Childhood Cognitive
  Development 70, 91
on women's health 3,
  85–86, 91
Bush, Prescott Sheldon 47

C
Card, Andrew 78
Carter, Jimmy 38
Cheney, Dick 64
CIT Credit Corporation 6
Clark, Mary Higgins 74
Clarke, John Clem 51
Clinton, Bill 46, 90
Clinton, Hillary Rodham 26,
  68

D
Department of Education, U.S.
  70
*Doak Walker: Three-Time All-
  American* 13, 88
Donnelly, Jan 30
Douglas, Michael D. "Mike"
  15–17, 88
Dykes, Judy 16

E
election (2000), presidential
  66–68
elementary school teachers.
  See teachers, elementary
  school
Experience Corps 11,
  55–56

F
Family Literacy Initiative, First
  Lady's 55–56, 70, 90

G

Gale, Linda 73
Gammon, Regan 28
Girl Scouts of the USA 10–11
Gnagy, Charlene 12, 24
Gore, Al 59, 65, 66, 67, 68
Grafton, Sue 74
Greater Texas Community Partners 84

H

Hance, Kent 37
Healthy Start, Grow Smart magazines 72
Heart Truth, The 85–86
Houston, Sam 51
Huey, Mary Page 56–57

I

Internet 93, 97, 125

J

Junior League 39

K

Kennedy, Edward 77
Kennedy, John F. 17, 77
King, Martin Luther Jr. 19
Klatt, Cindy Schumann 14

L

Language Enrichment Activities Program (LEAP) 71
Laura Bush Foundation for America's Libraries 76, 131
Lea, Tom 56
librarians
　advancement 121–122
　books about 126
　certification or licensing 116
　earnings 122–123
　employers 119–120
　exploring 117–118
　high school and postsecondary training 113–116
　job overview 107–113
　organizations and websites about 127–128
　outlook 124–125
　requirements 113–117
　starting out 120–121
　work environment 123–124
Library of Congress 73, 74
LoCastro, Andrea 93–94, 96, 99, 101, 102–103

M

Margaret Cone Center 71
Margo, Adair 56
Mauro, Gary 60
McCleskey, Robert 16, 17, 57, 58
McGovern, George 7
Mutombo, Dikembe 74

N

National Basketball Association 74
National Book Festival 73–76, 91
National Education Association 101–102, 104, 106
New Teacher Project 3, 71–72
New York magazine 65
New York Post 79
Nixon, Richard 7
No Child Left Behind (NCLB) Act 2, 69–70
Nowlin, Susan 21

O

O, The Oprah Magazine 6–7
O'Donnell, Lawrence Jr. 65
O'Neill, Jan Donnelly 7, 30, 31, 32
O'Neill, Joe 15, 30, 31, 58–59

P

Parent Teacher Organization 44
Patterson, James 76
People magazine 13
Putin, Vladimir 75
Putina, Lyudmila 75, 75
Putting Reading First initiative 78

Q

Quayle, Dan 44

R

Race for the Cure 86
Rainbow Rooms 84
Reach Out and Read 71
Reader's Digest 12
Reading First 70
Reading Rainbow (TV series) 74
Read to Achieve Program 74
Ready to Read, Ready to Learn 2, 56, 70–72, 90
Reagan, Ronald 38, 44
Red Dress Project 85–86, 91
Republican National Convention (2000) 1, 2, 11, *63,* 64, 91
Richards, Ann 47, 48–49, 50

S

San Jacinto Junior High School 14
Secret Service 78
Smith, Mrs. 10
Southern Methodist University (SMU) 13, 19, 21, 22, 51, 63, 64, 71, 88, 90, 131
Stine, R. L. 76
Supreme Court, United States 68, 91
Susan G. Komen Breast Cancer Foundation 86

T

Taliban 81, 82, 83
teachers, elementary school
    advancement 100–101
    books about 105–106
    certification or licensing 97–98

teachers, elementary school
(*continued*)
   earnings 101–102
   employers 99–100
   exploring 99
   high school and
     postsecondary training
     96–97
   job overview 92–96
   organizations and websites
     about 106
   outlook 103–104
   requirements 96–99
   starting out 100
   work environment 102–103
Teach for America 2–3, 71–72
terrorist attacks of 9/11 77–80, 91
Texas Book Festival 11, 73, 90
Texas Capitol Historical Art
   Committee 57
Texas Rangers 45
Transition to Teaching 71–72
Troops to Teachers 3, 71–72
Trout, Karen Thompson 14–15
Turow, Scott 74
Twain, Mark 76

U

University of Chicago 119
University of Texas 25–26, 43,
   52, 79, 89
Us Weekly magazine 79

W

Walker, Doak *14*, 19
Washington Post 79
Weiss, Peggy Porter 8
Welch, Harold 5, 6, 7, 20,
   22–23, 39, 42, 50, 57, 90
Welch, Jenna
   on daughter 5, 6, 8, 9,
     22–23, 33, 49, 57
   daughter on 6–7, 78
   grandchildren of 42
   on more children 39
   politics of 7
   on reading 11–13
Welch, Laura Lane 5. *See also*
   Bush, Laura Welch
Welch, Mark 23
White, Mark 73
"White House Salute to
   America's Authors" 76, 91
White House Summit on Early
   Childhood Cognitive
   Development 70, 91
White House website
   131
Winfrey, Oprah 6

Y

Yale University 43, 78

ABOUT THE AUTHOR

Dina E. Forbes received a bachelor of arts degree in English and journalism from Montclair State University in New Jersey. She has had several years of editing and writing experience in the field of English-language teaching (ELT). She has developed numerous English language teaching media, including print and CD materials, and has adapted several British ELT textbooks for the American English market. She has been involved with the development and production of classroom textbooks, audio scripts, workbooks, and ELT teacher-training manuals. Forbes volunteers for Literacy Volunteers of America, tutoring adult English as a second language (ESL) speakers. She has been a presenter at a number of language teaching conferences.